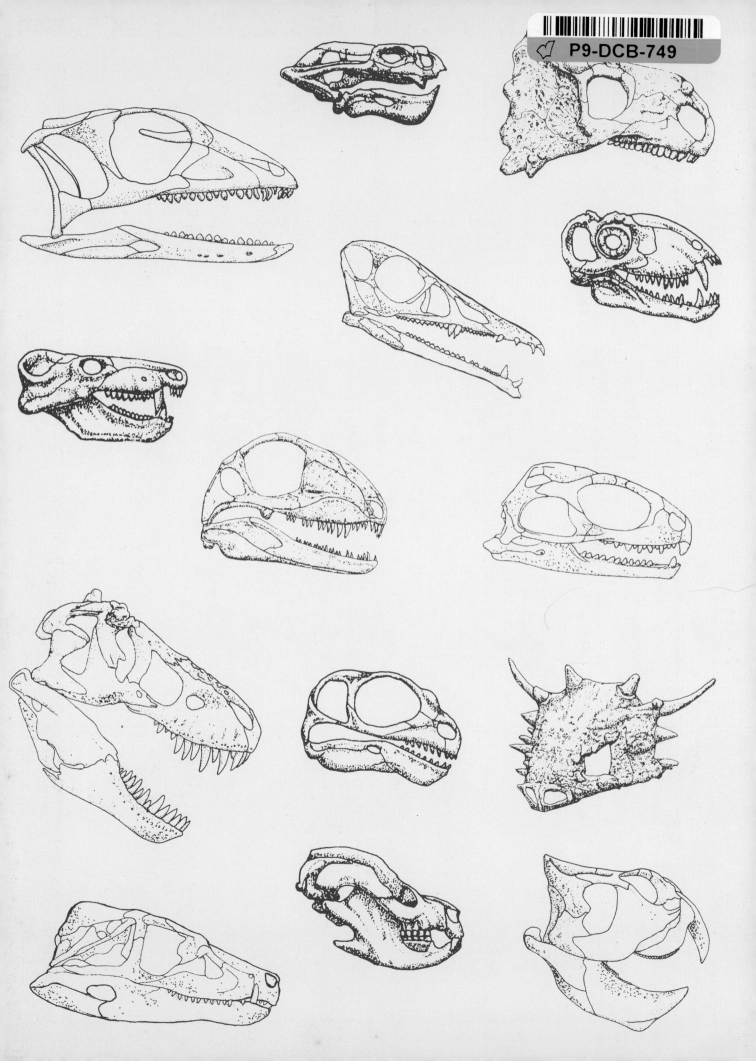

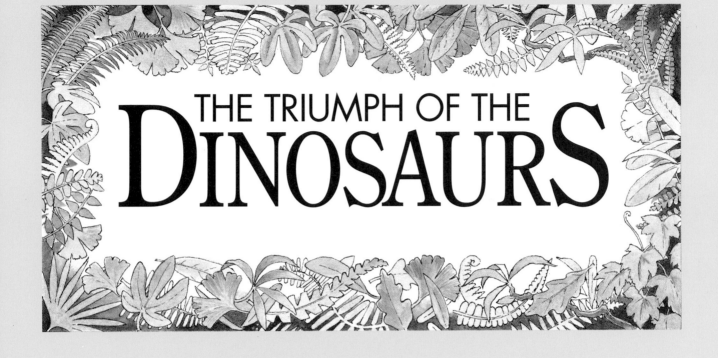

THE TRIUMPH OF THE
DINOSAURS

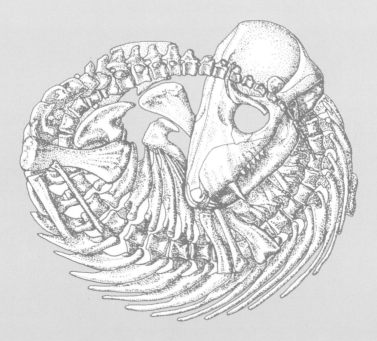

PICTURE CREDITS

The Author and the Publishers would like to thank
the following artists and photographers for their kind
permission to reproduce their paintings or
photographs in this book:

Brian Franczak: 18, 21, 26B, 33, 34, 36T, 37, 41B,
45, 62, 63B, 66, 80, 82;
John Gurche: 35, 85T;
Douglas Henderson: 16, 17, 19T, 32T, 51, 52–3,
58–9, 61, 63T, 70, 71T, 81, 84, 87, 89;
Natural History Museum Picture Library: 14, *15*,
19B, 20, *20–1*, *22–3*, 24, *24–25*, 26T, *27*, *28*, 29,
30–1, 32B, *38*, *39*, *41T*, *42–3*, 44, 46, *46–7*, 48–9
(both), 50–1, 52, 53, *54–5*, 56, 57, *60*, *64–5*, *68–9*,
71B, *72–3*, *74–5*, 75, 76, *77*, 78, *78–9*, *83*, 85B, 88;
Paintings listed as from the NHM Picture Library in
italic are by John Sibbick.
Dr David Norman: 67;
David Peters: 40.

The painting on the cover of this book is reproduced
by kind permission of the Natural History Museum
Picture Library and John Sibbick.

Skeleton and skull drawings by David Nicholls and
Denise Blagdon.
'Life on Earth' painting (pages 10–11) by Mr Gay
Galsworthy.
'Dinosaurs' Family Tree' (pages 12–13), page
borders and information box artwork by Adam
Marshall.

THE TRIUMPH OF THE
DINOSAURS

STEVE PARKER

Scientific Consultant:
DR DAVID NORMAN

DRAGON'S WORLD

CHILDREN'S BOOKS

Dragon's World Ltd
Limpsfield
Surrey RH8 0DY

First published by Dragon's World 1994

© 1994 Dragon's World Ltd

Editor: Diana Briscoe
Art Director: John Strange
Designer: Mel Raymond
DTP Manager: Keith Bambury
Editorial Director: Pippa Rubinstein

The catalogue record for this book
is available from the British Library.

ISBN 0 85028 228 5

Typeset by Dragon's World Ltd in Folio and Rockwell.
Printed in Hong Kong

CONTENTS

LIFE ON EARTH

There has been life on Earth for much of our planet's 4,600 million-year history. The first traces are microscopic fossils, over 3,500 million years old, of tiny life-forms resembling bacteria. For more than 1,500 million years, these were the only living things on our planet.

PRECAMBRIAN ERA

Cambrian Period: 590–505 mya

Ordovician Period: 505–438 mya

Silurian Period: 438–408 mya

Devonian Period: 408–360 mya

Carboniferous Period: 360–286 mya

Permian Period: 286–245 mya

PALEOZOIC ERA

Triassic Period: 245–205 mya

Jurassic Period: 205–144 mya

All numbers given are millions of years ago or mya

During the Paleozoic era, living things gradually became larger and more complicated. Shelled animals evolved over 500 million years ago (mya), followed by fishes. Then plants and animals, including insects and amphibians, invaded the land.

By the beginning of the Mesozoic era, life was well established on land. The first dinosaurs appeared over 210 million years ago. After their mysterious disappearance some 65 million years ago, mammals and birds took over the land during the Cenozoic era.

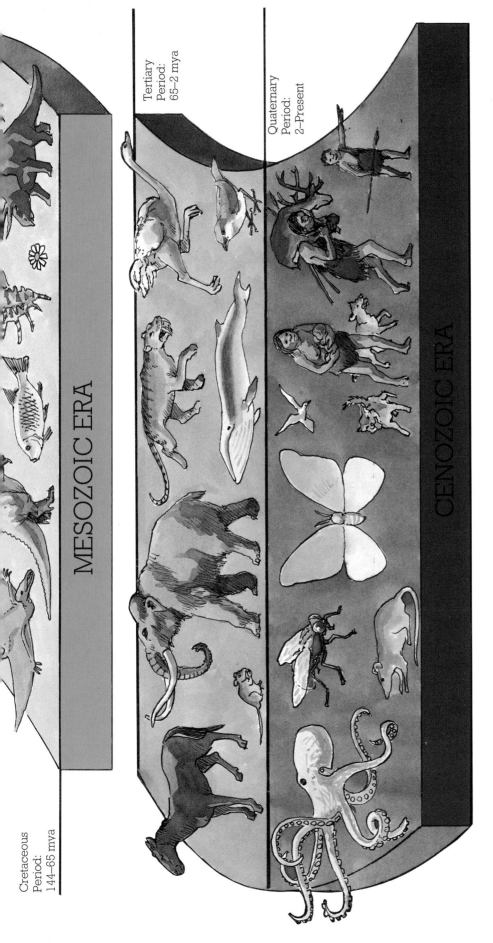

Cretaceous
Period:
144–65 mya

Tertiary
Period:
65–2 mya

Quaternary
Period:
2–Present

MESOZOIC ERA

CENOZOIC ERA

The vast time spans of prehistory are divided into main sections called eras. These are split, in turn, into periods.

The **Paleozoic** era, or 'ancient life', was dominated by creatures such as worms, jellyfishes, shelled sea animals, fishes, insects and amphibians. Many of these died out at the end of the Permian age.

Most of the next era, the **Mesozoic** or 'middle life', was the Age of Dinosaurs and Other Reptiles. Dinosaurs dominated the land, pterosaurs soared in the sky, while ichthyosaurs, mosasaurs and plesiosaurs swam through the seas.

The reptiles spread and diversified during the Triassic, the first period of the Mesozoic era. They reached their most gigantic during the Jurassic, and became more sophisticated during the Cretaceous.

The mass extinction of species at the end of the Cretaceous period was followed by the **Cenozoic** era, or 'recent life' – the Age of Mammals and Birds.

DINOSAURS' FAMILY TREE

This chart shows the dinosaur groups and how they came and went during the Mesozoic era (see pages 10–11).

Some flourished, but then died out, and others took their place. The whole dinosaur group is divided into two, on the basis of their hip bones:
- The Saurischians (or lizard-hipped dinosaurs) see pages 20–45;
- The Ornithischians (or bird-hipped dinosaurs) see pages 46–83.

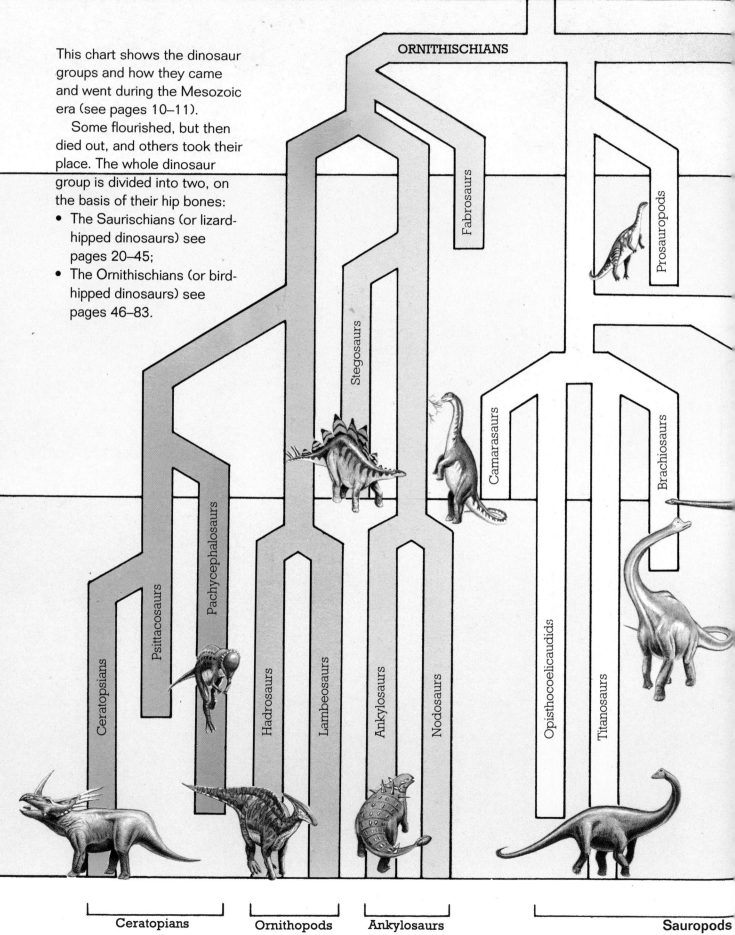

ORNITHISCHIANS

Fabrosaurs

Prosauropods

Stegosaurs

Camarasaurs

Brachiosaurs

Ceratopsians

Psittacosaurs

Pachycephalosaurs

Hadrosaurs

Lambeosaurs

Ankylosaurs

Nodosaurs

Opisthocoelicaudids

Titanosaurs

Ceratopians

Ornithopods

Ankylosaurs

Sauropods

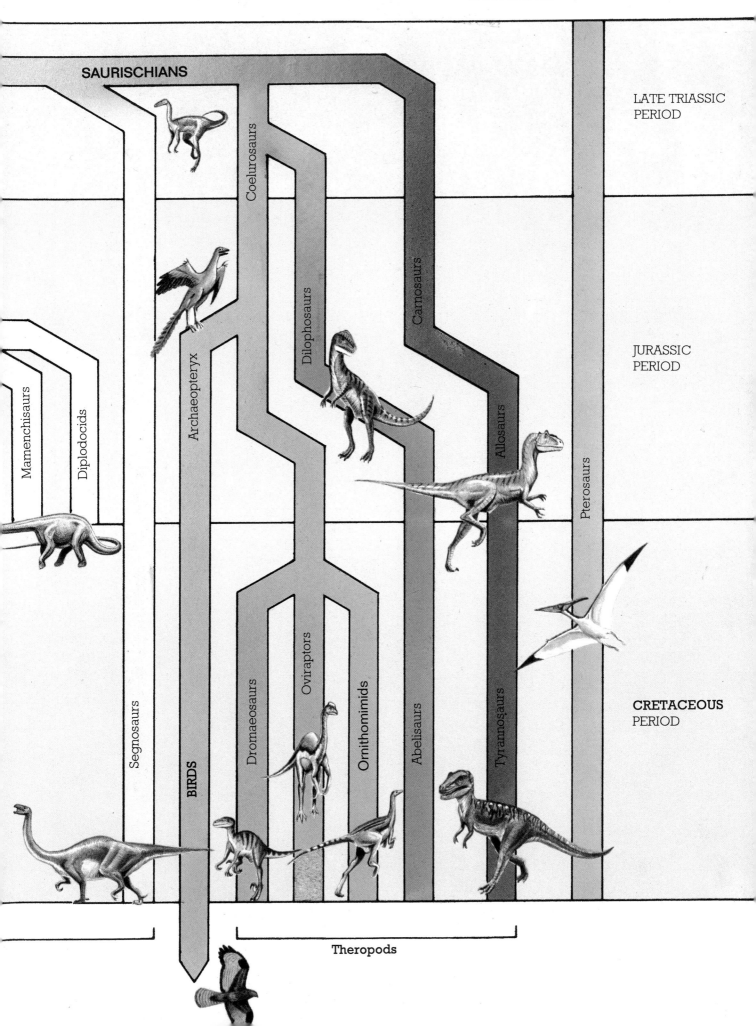

SAURISCHIANS

LATE TRIASSIC PERIOD

JURASSIC PERIOD

CRETACEOUS PERIOD

Coelurosaurs

Archaeopteryx

Mamenchisaurs

Diplodocids

Dilophosaurs

Carnosaurs

Allosaurs

Pterosaurs

Segnosaurs

BIRDS

Dromaeosaurs

Oviraptors

Ornithomimids

Abelisaurs

Tyrannosaurs

Theropods

HOW DINOSAURS LIVED

Our knowledge of dinosaurs comes from two main sources. One is fossils – their bones, teeth, claws, horns, eggs, skin, droppings, footprints and so on, turned to stone. The other main source is our knowledge of living animals – how they grow, feed, battle with rivals, mate, raise young, chase, get chased, and eventually die. By using the two sources, we can imagine what a dinosaur looked like, and also guess how it lived and behaved in the prehistoric landscape.

Rebuilding the past

Ecology is one of the newest sciences. It deals with animals and plants and how they relate to each other – who eats what, where they live, and why. Its aim is to build up a complete picture of what happens in nature, and to understand the principles by which nature works.

As we study ecology in today's world, we can use what we learn to imagine the ecology of the prehistoric world. This is the fascinating subject of paleo-ecology. It allows us to take dinosaurs whose bodies have been 're-built' from fossils, and almost bring them to life. We can suggest where and how they lived, how they fed and bred – in other words, what they did all day.

▲ This scene from the Cretaceous period, 100 million years ago, includes mosses, ferns, horsetails, cycads (a sort of palm), cypresses, and the relatively new flowers and broad-leaved trees. Then, as now, plants were the basic food for all animals.

◄ It was thought that the small bird-hipped *Hypsilophodon* lived in trees. But another look at its fossil foot bones, and comparison with the ecology of today's animals, makes this unlikely (see page 46).

Herbivores and carnivores

One part of ecology is the study of feeding relationships. Animals that eat meat are called carnivores. Plant-eating animals are called herbivores. Animals that hunt other animals are predators; their victims are prey. There must always be more prey than predators, otherwise the predators would run out of food.

As most prey is herbivorous, we know that the herbivorous dinosaurs must have outnumbered the carnivorous ones. This type of ecological work helps us to re-create the prehistoric landscape, with its plants, dinosaurs and other animal inhabitants.

DINOSAUR BEHAVIOUR

Clues from fossils

Fossils tell us about dinosaur bodies and about dinosaur behaviour. Fossilized footprints can be very informative. Their size and shape tell us which kind of dinosaur made them. Their depth in the ground and distance apart tell us something about the

▼ Two pterosaurs fly over a herd of sauropod dinosaurs walking on the mud of a dried-up river. millions of years ago. Many sauropod footprints were preserved and have been found as fossils.

weight of the dinosaur and its stride – whether it was walking or running. Many footprints found close together were probably made at the same time. This shows us that some dinosaurs walked together in groups, and suggests that they lived in herds. From our knowledge of herd-living animals today, we can assume that dinosaurs probably had a social structure and communicated with each other. Many examples of trackways made by huge sauropod (see page 38) dinosaurs have been found.

Parental care

The crocodiles of today are close relatives of dinosaurs. The female crocodile lays her eggs in warm soil on a riverbank. When the babies hatch, she helps them from the shells, carries them to water, and guards them fiercely. Fossil finds suggest that some dinosaurs also cared for their babies. Fossilized nests containing eggs and newly hatched dinosaurs have been found in which the youngsters had worn teeth. This indicates that they must have had food to chew, and this was probably brought to them by their mother. This is a fascinating glimpse into dinosaur family life.

▼ The hadrosaur *Maiasaura* watches her new babies in their nest. Preserved eggs and babies of this dinosaur give clues about parental behaviour in dinosaurs.

DINOSAUR FOOD

Few things in life are more important than food. A dinosaur's jaws, teeth and other feeding parts tell us a great deal about what it ate, and following from this, about its lifestyle. We know if it was a herbivore or a carnivore, if it was a selective feeder or ate a wide variety of foods, and if it was a hunter or one of the hunted.

Tooth design

A lion has sharp, pointed teeth for tearing and ripping flesh, and sharp claws to slash victims. A zebra has broad, flat-topped teeth for grinding grasses and other plant material, and slim legs with light hooves for running away. These two basic types of feeding method are found in predators

▲ *Coelophysis bauri* had long, sharp teeth with serrated edges, like a saw. They were ideal for cutting and slicing the flesh of its prey. Its long hand claws were designed for scratching, grabbing and slashing the prey.

and prey throughout the animal world. They were present in dinosaur times too. Dinosaurs with sharp, pointed teeth were carnivorous flesh-eaters. Those with wide, broad-topped teeth were plant-chewers.

Other food clues

The size of a dinosaur is another indication as to what it ate. A large hunter such as *Tyrannosaurus* would probably have fed on large victims. It may have killed prey itself, or scavenged – eaten animals already dead. Smaller carnivores would have chased smaller prey such as lizards and insects.

Some herbivores, especially the giant sauropods, had tiny teeth like pegs or prongs. These would have been useful for stripping leaves off twigs and raking in vegetation. These dinosaurs could not chew. It is thought that they had huge stomachs, where their plant food rotted into a more easily digestible paste. Pebbles have been found with the bones of sauropods. The dinosaurs may have swallowed them to grind their food.

▲ A tyrannosaur-type dinosaur uses its sharp jagged-edged teeth, strong jaws and powerful neck muscles to tear flesh from the carcass of a horned dinosaur.

▼ Stomach stones from the preserved remains of a sauropod dinosaur. These are called 'gastroliths' and were worn smooth by rubbing and grinding plant food. The largest is over 7 centimetres long.

MEAT-EATERS

Dinosaurs are divided into two groups called lizard-hipped (saurischians) and bird-hipped (ornithischians – see page 46). There were two groups of lizard-hipped dinosaurs – theropods and sauropodomorphs (see page 38). Theropods were meat-eating dinosaurs. They stood on their back legs, had strong claws and sharp teeth.

'Beast-feet'

The theropods included all of the meat-eating or carnivorous dinosaurs, from the tiny *Compsognathus* to the largest-ever land carnivore, *Tyrannosaurus*. The word theropod means 'beast-foot'. It describes these dinosaurs' three-toed feet, each toe tipped with a sharp claw, typical of a predator.

There are several groups of theropods: the varied ceratosaurs such as *Dilophosaurus*; the slim, light coelurosaurs such as *Ornithomimus*; the large carnosaurs such as *Tyrannosaurus* and *Allosaurus*; and the 'odd theropods' such as the huge-clawed *Baryonyx*, which are included here because they do not seem to fit into any of the other groups.

▼ *Stegosaurus* (see page 82) was another Jurassic ornithischian, like *Kentrosaurus*, but it lived in North America. Like all ornithischians, it was a plant-eater.

▲ This is the fossil skeleton of the theropod *Coelophysis*. It has the bones of an even smaller *Coelophysis* inside it. This suggests that it might have been a cannibal.

▶ *Kentrosaurus* (see pages 80–81) was a Jurassic ornithischian. It was a stegosaur (plated dinosaur) that lived in Africa.

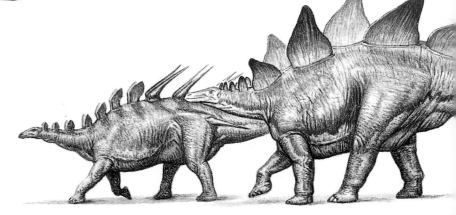

▲ *Dilophosaurus* grew to about 6 metres long.
It was one of the ceratosaur group of theropods
(see page 23).

▼ *Yangchuanosaurus* was a Jurassic saurischian.
It was a member of the carnosaur theropod
subgroup, a fierce meat-eater like *Allosaurus*.
Its fossils come from China.

◄ *Brachiosaurus* (see page
40) was another Jurassic
saurischian. It belonged to the
sauropod subgroup of huge
plant-eaters. This animal was
the largest of all the well-
studied dinosaurs, and lived in
North America and Africa.

A strange reptile

One of the best-known theropods is *Allosaurus*, from the carnosaur group. It lived in North America towards the end of the Jurassic period, around 150–140 million years ago. At 12 metres long, it was the largest predator of its time. The name *Allosaurus* means 'strange reptile'. It was called this because the first of its fossils to be found were scarce, and for a while they were confused with the remains of other dinosaurs.

Giant fangs

Allosaurus had a huge head, with a skull that was almost 1 metre long. The jaws were equipped with rows of fearsome teeth longer than your fingers. These curved backwards, like hooks, so that a struggling victim could not escape. The teeth edges were serrated like a saw, for shearing through flesh. *Allosaurus* had strong arms with huge hooked claws on its fingers, to hold down and rip up prey.

Its powerful back legs had massive claws too. The first of the four toes pointed backwards, and was relatively short, so that it even with its horny claw, it hardly touched the ground. The other three toes pointed forwards and were broad and long. They would have spread the weight of this large, heavy animal, to prevent *Allosaurus* sinking into soft ground. There is further information on this supreme flesh-eater on page 28.

Bump on the nose

At the same time as *Allosaurus*, and in the same place, lived a similar but smaller theropod called *Ceratosaurus*. It was 6 metres long from nose-tip to tail-tip. It had rows of sharp teeth in its mouth, like *Allosaurus*, but they were not so large or numerous.

One curious feature of *Ceratosaurus* was the strange, bony lump on the end of its snout. This does not seem to have been a weapon. It may have been a sign of size and maturity which *Ceratosaurus* used to impress mates and rivals. Rhinoceroses today display their nose-horns when they battle to win mates, and when they chase intruding rhinoceroses from their territory.

▼ The slicing, stabbing teeth of *Allosaurus* would have ripped into prey such as the plated dinosaur *Stegosaurus*, the ornithopod *Camptosaurus* and the huge sauropod *Apatosaurus*. These were all contemporaries of *Allosaurus* in North America during the late Jurassic period.

▼ When *Allosaurus* lived in North America, the first known bird was flying in Europe. This was *Archaeopteryx* (see page 84).

▼ The teeth and jaws of *Dilophosaurus* were not particularly large or strong. This dinosaur may have been a scavenger, picking meat from dead carcasses.

▲ *Ceratosaurus* had four fingers on each hand, unlike many of its theropod relatives which had three.

▲ *Allosaurus* had strong, pillar-shaped back legs. It was a large animal, and some small prey would have been able to dodge its claws and jaws.

Crests on the head

Dilophosaurus was a ceratosaur theropod, like *Ceratosaurus.* It was the first of the big meat-eating dinosaurs, and lived about 190 million years ago in western North America. It is named 'two-ridged reptile' because of the curious ridges or crests on its skull, like two halves of a dinner plate stuck on its head. As with the nose-bump of *Ceratosaurus*, these may have been signs of age and maturity.

A mixed bunch

The coelurosaurs had various body features in common. But this does not mean that they were all closely related to each other. They are a 'mixed bag' of dinosaurs. They are grouped together because of their similarities, and for our convenience, rather than because they formed a family grouping in nature. The same may also be true of other theropod groups.

One of the original coelurosaurs, and one of the earliest of all dinosaurs, was *Coelophysis*. Some experts say that *Coelophysis* would be better included in the ceratosaur group (see page 22) rather than in the coelurosaur group. This type of discussion is made even more interesting as new evidence may come to light any time.

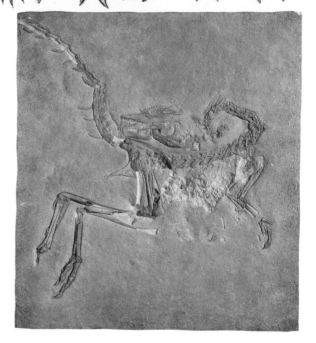

▲ This skeleton of *Compsognathus* from Bavaria, Germany, is preserved in incredible detail. It even has the remains of the dinosaur's last meal, a small lizard, fossilized with it.

▶ *Ornitholestes* (in the background) could have torn bones and flesh from the dead bodies of larger dinosaurs.

Fossils galore

Coelophysis is one of the most-studied of all dinosaurs. This is because fossil-hunters discovered lots of preserved skeletons at a place called Ghost Ranch in New Mexico, USA. It is thought that the animals may have been swept to their death by a sudden flood.

Coelophysis was 3 metres long and stood almost as tall as an adult human. Its long, slim legs show that it was a fast runner. Its hands had long claws for grabbing prey. Its teeth were sharp and saw-edged, and its mouth was long and low. These features point to a creature that could run, jump, twist and turn at speed, and snatch and bite any small animal that it could catch – including smaller dinosaurs.

Mini-dinosaur

One of the smallest of all dinosaurs was *Compsognathus*, or 'pretty jaw'. Even with its long neck and tail, it was only 1 metre long, and its body was little larger than a human hand. This tiny creature terrorized insects, lizards and other small creatures in Europe about 140 million years ago.

We have good evidence for this (see opposite), because one skeleton of *Compsognathus* was fossilized with an even smaller skeleton in the place where its stomach would have been. The smaller animal was a lizard – called *Bavarisaurus* – the *Compsognathus*'s last supper.

Ornitholestes was another coelurosaur, also from about 140 million years ago. It is known from only one partial set of fossil bones discovered in 1900 in Wyoming, USA. *Ornitholestes* had strong fingers and large teeth, and may have tackled larger prey, such as larger lizards and baby dinosaurs. Its name means 'bird robber', from an old idea that it snatched birds out of their nests.

◀ There would have been plenty of mini-victims for *Coelophysis* to hunt, including lizards, amphibians, insects such as dragonflies, worms and very early, shrew-like mammals.

▲ *Compsognathus* probably ran on its back legs with its body leaning forward, so that its head and neck balanced its tail at the back.

◀ The long flexible neck of *Coelophysis* meant that this dinosaur could dart its head about, snapping at prey.

Puzzles and questions

Many dinosaurs are represented by fossils of only small pieces, such as a few teeth, a piece of skull bone, or a foot. It is fascinating for scientists to work out which fossils belong together, and what these dinosaurs were like.

The 'odd theropods' are another mixed bunch of dinosaurs, known from scarce and puzzling remains. They do not seem to fit neatly into the other groups of theropods – the ceratosaurs, coelurosaurs and carnosaurs.

One of these odd theropods is *Baryonyx*, named after its massive 'heavy claw'. This is one of the most recent dinosaurs to have been discovered. Its fossils were unearthed in a clay pit in Surrey, England, in 1982–83. This dinosaur had a long, low skull, not unlike a crocodile, with rows of large teeth at the front, and smaller peg-like teeth behind. It seems that each of its hands was armed with a huge curving claw, bigger than your entire hand. *Baryonyx* may have fed on fish, which it hooked out of the water with its finger-claw and grasped in its sharp front teeth before chewing it.

▼ This skeleton of *Baryonyx* was preserved in the rocks for about 125 million years.

▼ *Baryonyx walkeri* charges through a swamp hunting prey. It may also used its massive finger-claw to hook fish out of the water.

Small predators

Segnosaur fossils were first discovered in the 1970s in Mongolia. These seem to be the remains of several kinds of dinosaur.

Segnosaurus was 5–7 metres long, with a toothless 'beak' at the front of its jaw and small, pointed teeth behind. It may have eaten fish.

Segisaurus was a small theropod in western North America 190 million years ago. It was probably a predator of about 1 metre long, perhaps similar to the coelurosaurs. The head was missing from the fossil skeleton, so we do not know.

Avimimus was another puzzling creature. Its fossils come from Mongolia and date from near the end of the Age of Dinosaurs, about 70 million years ago (see also page 86). From the tiny bumps on its arm bones, it may have had feathers, like a bird.

Segnosaurus

Say it: Sayg-no–sore-us
Dinosaur group: Segnosaur (?Theropoda, Saurischia)
When it lived: 80–70 million years ago, in the late Cretacious period
Where it lived: Mongolia in Asia
Approx. size: Length 5–7 metres, height 2–3 metres
Special features: Mouth had a toothless, horny beak at the front and small pointed teeth behind; only a few fossils found, so not a well known species

▼ These three theropods are *Segnosaurus* on the left (rebuilt from several sets of remains), *Segisaurus* below, and *Avimimus* on the right.

More carnosaurs

Here we look in more detail at the carnosaur theropods, and how they might have hunted or scavenged their meals.

The fossilized teeth and jawbone of *Megalosaurus* caused great interest when their discovery was first announced. This was more than a century and a half ago, in 1824. In fact, *Megalosaurus* was the very first dinosaur to be described and named in a scientific article. The article was written by animal and fossil expert William Buckland of Oxford University, England. The second was *Iguanodon* (see page 52).

Megalosaurus means 'mega (really big) reptile'. It was not called a dinosaur, because the name had not been invented yet. The word was coined by another fossil expert, Richard Owen of London, in 1842 (see page 53). Buckland thought that his creature could have been an elephant-sized predatory lizard. But he was puzzled by the apparent great age of the rocks in which the fossils were embedded.

Allosaurus (see also page 22) was another typical carnosaur and a fearsome predator.

▲ Gaps in the skull of *Allosaurus* make it lighter. The sixty or so dagger-like teeth would have sliced easily through meat.

▼ This *Allosaurus* is attacking a young *Diplodocus* (see page 42). After causing serious wounds, the carnosaur would wait until the sauropod bled to death.

Lots of teeth

The fossils of *Megalosaurus* are from rocks of the late Jurassic period, around 140 million years ago. The first fossils were found in Oxfordshire, England. Several other sets of fossils that could be *Megalosaurus* have also been found in other areas. They suggest a large theropod about 8 metres long, similar in general shape to carnosaurs like *Allosaurus*.

The jawbone had the long, backwards-curving, saw-edged teeth typical of the theropods. It also had small teeth inside the jawbone. These would have gradually pushed out and replaced the older, worn ones. They show how dinosaurs always had new sets of teeth growing.

Saving weight

Big dinosaurs had to carry a lot of weight. Some of the carnosaurs had features that helped to reduce this. Holes in *Allosaurus's* skull made it less heavy, yet almost as strong. The holes also allowed the jaw muscles to work more effectively and bulge as they pulled on the jaws.

▲ The fossil jawbone and teeth of the 'big reptile' *Megalosaurus*. You can see the small, new teeth which gradually grew and replaced the old ones.

▼ This is the fossil skeleton of *Gasosaurus*, a small carnosaur. It was about 2 metres tall and 4 metres long. It hunted in China, 160 million years ago.

Fast hunters

The dromaeosaurs, or 'running reptiles', walked on their two back legs, and were about as tall as humans. Some experts put them in the coelurosaur subgroup of theropods, while others put them in their own theropod group. Whatever the view, the dromaeosaurs were some of the most exciting and frightening of all the hunting dinosaurs. Fossils of some dromaeosaurs have been found in groups, with the preserved bones of several individuals jumbled together. This suggests that they lived and hunted in packs, like wolves do today.

The skull and teeth of *Dromaeosaurus* itself have been found as fossils, but most of the rest of the body can only be rebuilt using information from the fossils of its dromaeosaur cousins. One type, *Velociraptor,* meaning 'speedy thief', was about 2 metres long. Another type was the 3-metre-long *Deinonychus*, meaning 'terrible claw'.

▶ *Deinonychus* was about 3 metres long from nose to tail. Its fossils date from the mid Cretaceous period, about 100 million years ago, and have been found in western North America.

The clawed killers

The most noticeable feature of a dromaeosaur is the curved claw on the second toe of each foot. While the dinosaur was walking, this claw was held up clear of the ground, to prevent it becoming worn and blunt. When the dinosaur attacked, it would kick out with its leg and flick the huge claw around in a curve, like a slashing knife. In this way, the dromaeosaur could rip open smaller prey on its own. Several of these predatory dinosaurs together could attack a large victim and gash deep wounds in it, so that it became weak from loss of blood.

▲ Only a few fossils of *Dromaeosaurus* have been found – in the late Cretaceous rocks of western North America. Note the large claw on each second toe.

▼ *Deinonychus* holds its terrible foot claw up and out of the way, as it runs after a victim. The claw is ready to swing down like the blade of a meat-slicer.

Deinonychus

Say it: Day-non-ick-us
Dinosaur group: Dromaeosaur (Theropoda, Saurischia)
When it lived: 100 million years ago, in the mid Cretaceous period
Where it lived: Montana, North America
Approx. size: Length 3 metres, height 1.5–2 metres, weight 70 kg
Special features: Large skull and brain-case; second toe equipped with large, swinging claw; strong hands with powerful fingers

▲ *Velociraptor* lived about 80–70 million years ago in Mongolia. In one fossil find it seems to be grappling with a small horned dinosaur, *Protoceratops* (see page 68).

Ostrich-dinosaurs

The ornithomimosaurs, or 'bird-mimic reptiles', were theropod dinosaurs from late in the Cretaceous period, around 70 million years ago. They are known by the nickname of 'ostrich-dinosaurs'. If you look at their reconstructions here, you can see that they had many features that were similar to the ostrich, the largest bird living today.

Ornithomimosaurs had a long, beak-like mouth with no teeth. They had long, muscular back legs and were about 2 metres high – all features that are similar to those of the ostrich. Including their slim, flexible neck, and long, balancing tail, ornithomimosaurs were about 3–4 metres long.

▲ The ostrich-dinosaurs, like this *Struthiomimus* from North America, had large eyes in a small head. They probably hunted mainly by sight. *Struthiomimus* means 'ostrich mimic'.

▼ *Gallimimus*, the 'chicken mimic', was an ostrich-dinosaur from Mongolia. It was about 4 metres long from the tip of its nose to the end of its tail.

Ostrich comparisons

By comparing the ostrich-dinosaurs with real ostriches, we can make two good guesses about their behaviour. First, the ostrich-dinosaurs were extremely fast, strong runners. An ostrich-dinosaur such as *Struthiomimus* might have raced along at more than 50 kilometres per hour. Their bones were slim and light, and had large, roughened areas where powerful muscles were attached.

Second, it's likely that these dinosaurs snapped up all types of small food items in their 'beaks'. But they had no teeth, so they could not chew or cut off large pieces of food. They probably fed on worms, insects, small amphibians, reptiles and mammals, and perhaps plant matter such as soft leaves, buds, seeds and fruits. The ostrich has a similar wide and varied menu. A creature that eats all kinds of food – plants as well as animals – is called an omnivore.

▲ *Chirostenotes pergracilis* was a late-Cretaceous dinosaur from North America. It is known from only very few fossils. It may have been an ostrich-dinosaur, or a dromaeosaur (see pages 30–31), or even a coelurosaur (see pages 24–25).

▼ *Ornithomimus altus* shows the similarity in body shape and proportions to the living bird, the ostrich. Ostrich-dinosaurs lived right to the end of the Age of Dinosaurs, about 65 million years ago.

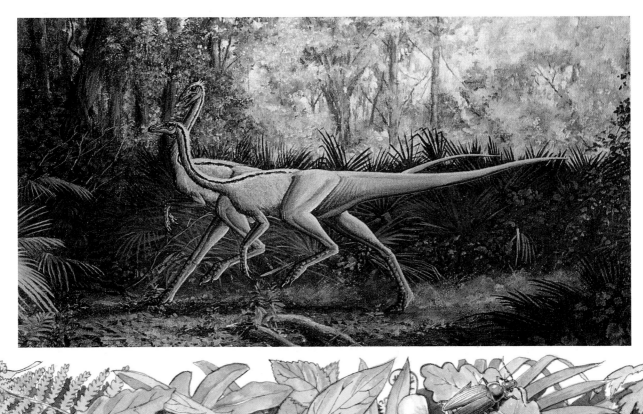

King of the meat-eaters

The last main group of theropod dinosaurs is the carnosaurs, or 'meat-eating reptiles'. A sub-group is the tyrannosaurs, or the 'tyrant reptiles'. This group contains possibly the most famous dinosaur of all – the huge *Tyrannosaurus,* sometimes called *Tyrannosaurus rex*, 'king of the tyrant reptiles'. Few victims escaped its mouthful of razor-sharp teeth, each as long as a steak knife. These teeth were clamped together using enormously powerful jaw muscles. There were several other huge flesh-eaters in this group of carnosaurs. They all lived at the very end of the Age of Dinosaurs, about 65 million years ago, in western North America and eastern Asia.

Tyrannosaurus

Say it: Tie-ran-oh-sore-us
Dinosaur group: Carnosaur (Theropoda, Saurischia)
When it lived: 70–65 mya, in the late Cretaceous
Where it lived: Alberta, Montana, Texas and other sites in North America; possibly Mongolia in Asia
Approx. size: Length 15 metres, height 6 metres, weight 7 tonnes
Special features: The biggest land meat-eater ever on Earth; huge teeth; massively powerful neck and back legs

▼ *Nanotyrannus lancensis* is a 'mini' version of the great *Tyrannosaurus*. Small versions of animals have appeared through the ages, especially on distant islands. There have been dwarf dinosaurs, dwarf birds, dwarf hippos and even dwarf elephants.

▶ The smallest and biggest – a tiny ornithomimosaur tries to escape from the huge three-clawed foot of the largest therapod *Tyrannosaurus*. Note the small, seemingly useless arms of *Tyrannosaurus*.

The tyrannosaurs

The tyrannosaurs include *Albertosaurus* and *Daspletosaurus* from North America, and *Tarbosaurus* from eastern Asia. There are also fossils of tyrannosaur-type dinosaurs from India and South America. *Tyrannosaurus* itself was a massive beast. It was over 6 metres high, 15 metres long, and weighed over 7 tonnes – almost three times as much as an adult elephant. *Tarbosaurus* was about 12–13 metres long. *Albertosaurus* and *Daspletosaurus* were about 9 metres long.

◄ This skeleton of *Albertosaurus* shows the powerful back legs and tiny arms, typical of the tyrannosaurs.

▲ *Albertosaurus* prowls in the woods in the late Cretaceous period. It sniffs for food, and listens for the sound of prey.

Albertosaurus

Say it: Al-bert-oh-sore-us
Dinosaur group: Carnosaur (Theropoda, Saurischia)
When it lived: 80–70 million years ago, in the late Cretaceous period
Where it lived: Alberta in North America
Approx. size: Length 8 metres, height 3–4 metres, weight 2–3 tonnes
Special features: Lightly built for active pursuit of prey; large claws on feet for stabbing kicks

Getting a meal

Tyrannosaurus was the largest predator ever to walk on Earth. But there has been a long-running discussion among dinosaur experts about how it actually caught its prey. Theories have changed as we have learned more about these huge creatures.

Many years ago it was thought that this dinosaur was a scavenger which turned up after other carnivores had made a kill, driving them away and ripping up the body for itself. Then it was thought that it was a fast runner and could keep up the chase until its prey dropped from exhaustion.

Now the popular view is that *Tyrannosaurus* was a stealthy ambusher, which charged from the cover of trees, taking its victim by surprise and jabbing its sharp teeth into the body. It could have charged fast over a short distance and killed a dinosaur, such as a hadrosaur (see pages 56–57), using its powerful jaws and neck, and sharp teeth.

Daspletosaurus

Say it: Daz-plett-oh-sore-us
Dinosaur group: Carnosaur (Theropoda, Saurischia)
When it lived: 80–70 million years ago, in the late Cretaceous period
Where it lived: Alberta, North America
Approx. size: Length 8 metres, height 3–4 metres, weight 3–4 tonnes
Special features: Fewer but larger teeth (up to 15 cm long) than similar-sized carnosaurs

▼ Two *Daspletosaurus torosus* attack an armoured dinosaur called *Panoplosaurus* (see page 76). *Daspletosaurus* had very strong teeth and jaws.

GIANTS OF THE PAST

The second great group of lizard-hipped dinosaurs is the sauropodomorphs, or 'reptile-feet'. Most were huge sauropods with small heads, very long necks and tails, tubby bodies and thick legs. Prosauropods came earlier – they were smaller and more compact.

Giants of the Jurassic

The sauropods are many people's idea of a typical dinosaur. Most of these giants thundered across the land during the middle and late Jurassic period, about 160–140 million years ago. Most of them had no obvious armour or weapons. It seems that their main defence was their size and weight, and perhaps their herd-dwelling lifestyle. Recent discoveries show that some sauropods lived until the end of the Cretaceous period, right at the end of the Age of Dinosaurs. Some of these had protective plates of bone 'armour' embedded in their skin, or had heavy tail-clubs (see page 45).

▼ *Anchisaurus* scurries along the ground, while *Plateosaurus* reaches up for higher food. Fossils of *Anchisaurus* come from eastern North America and southern Africa. *Plateosaurus* lived in Europe.

▲ Some true sauropods of 180 million years ago. From the left: *Vulcanodon*, *Saltasaurus* and *Opisthocoelicaudia*.

The prosauropods

These small to medium-sized dinosaurs appeared fairly early in the Age of Dinosaurs, about 200 million years ago. They were the forerunners of the huge sauropods of 40–60 million years later. We cannot say for sure if the prosauropods were the true ancestors of the later sauropods. More fossil finds may answer this question.

It is thought that the early dinosaurs, such as *Coelophysis* (see page 24), stood on two legs and were small, agile carnivores. The prosauropods were probably the first dinosaurs that differed from this pattern. They evolved a large body and became plant-eaters. The first dinosaur of any real size was the prosauropod *Plateosaurus*, at 8 metres long. It could walk on all-fours, or rear up on its back legs to reach leaves and shoots. *Anchisaurus* was a smaller prosauropod about 2.5 metres long.

Plateosaurus

Say it: Platt-ee-oh-sore-us
Dinosaur group: Plateosaurid (Prosauropoda, Saurischia)
When it lived: 210–190 mya, during the late Triassic and early Jurassic
Where it lived: Western Europe
Approx. size: Length 8 metres, height 4 metres (rearing up on back legs), weight 5–7 tonnes
Special features: The first truly large dinosaur; probably lived in herds

Tallest of all

The biggest dinosaurs belonged to the brachiosaur-type group of sauropods. *Brachiosaurus* was a vast creature some 23 metres long with a great neck and very long front legs. Its name means 'arm reptile'.

It could browse on leaves more than 12 metres above the ground – that's twice as high as a modern giraffe can reach. With its bulky body and immense column-shaped legs it had a total body weight of perhaps 40 tonnes – about the same as one giant juggernaut lorry. Fossils of *Brachiosaurus* have been unearthed in Colorado, USA, and also in Tanzania, Africa.

Despite its great size, *Brachiosaurus* was probably a peaceful plant-eater. It had rows of small, chisel-shaped teeth in its jaws, which were suited to tearing and snipping off leaves and other plant material. To feed its enormous bulk, *Brachiosaurus* must have spent most of the day eating.

Brachiosaurus

Say it: Brack-ee-oh-sore-us
Dinosaur group: Brachiosaurid (Sauropoda, Saurischia)
When it lived: 150–130 mya, in the late Jurassic and early Cretaceous
Where it lived: Colorado, North America; Algeria and Tanzania, Africa
Approx. size: Length 23 metres, height 12 metres, weight 35–40 tonnes
Special features: Front legs longer than rear legs, so the body sloped from head to tail

▼ A *Brachiosaurus* family walks by a lake. This sauropod had unusually long front legs, and nostrils on top of its head.

Bigger still?

Despite its gigantic size, *Brachiosaurus* may not have been the biggest dinosaur. Fossil bones have been found that could belong to even larger sauropods. These have been called *Supersaurus*, *Ultrasaurus* and *Seismosaurus*. The bones do not form complete skeletons, and they are still being studied. But it is possible that *Seismosaurus* was over 35 metres long and weighed more than 50 tonnes. This would make *Seismosaurus* the largest animal ever to have lived on land.

   Camarasaurus was similar to *Brachiosaurus* but slightly smaller, at about 18 metres long. It also had strong, chisel-shaped teeth, in contrast to the next group of sauropods, the diplodocids, described on the following pages.

▼ The first fossils of *Camarasaurus* were discovered at the Dinosaur National Monument, Utah, USA, in 1925.

▼ During the late Jurassic period, *Seismosaurus hallorum* strolls across a drying lake-bed in what is now New Mexico, USA.

A huge mistake

If you ask someone to name a few very large dinosaurs, he or she may well include *Brontosaurus* in the list. But there is now no dinosaur with the official name of *Brontosaurus*. There used to be one, but experts realized that its fossils had been muddled with those of similar sauropods such as *Diplodocus* and *Camarasaurus*. To clear up the confusion, it was agreed that the dinosaur previously known by the name of *Brontosaurus*, the 'thunder reptile', would be called *Apatosaurus*, or 'deceptive

reptile'. So that is why the name *Brontosaurus* has disappeared from the official list of dinosaur names.

But this does not alter the fact that *Apatosaurus* was a huge dinosaur, 21 metres long and weighing up to 35 tonnes. It belonged to a group of sauropods called the diplodocids, after *Diplodocus*, the 'double-beam reptile'.

▼ *Diplodocus* lived in western North America at the end of the Jurassic period, about 140 million years ago. Its long tail accounted for more than half of its overall length. Its head was only 60 centimetres long.

Diplodocus holds the record for the longest of all the dinosaurs, at more than 27 metres. It may lose this record when we know more about sauropods such as *Seismosaurus* (see page 41). *Diplodocus* had a relatively slim body and legs. Its total weight was probably about 10–12 tonnes. This was light compared to some other dinosaurs.

Pencils for teeth

The diplodocids had tiny heads, and blunt teeth shaped like pencils or fingers. The teeth were clustered in a fringe at the front of the mouth and were probably used as rakes to pull leaves and other plant parts from their twigs and stems. These dinosaurs had no chewing teeth. They swallowed food whole and relied on stomach stones (see page 19) to mash it up in the stomach. Remains have been discovered at several sites in mid-western and central North America.

◀ *Apatosaurus* had broad, flat feet like those of an elephant. This meant its great weight was spread over a larger area, stopping it from sinking into soft earth. Its remains have been discovered at several sites in the mid-western and central North America.

The longest neck

Diplodocus may have been the longest dinosaur but the longest neck belonged to *Mamenchisaurus*, a sauropod from late Jurassic times. It was named after Mamenchi in China, where it was discovered.

Brachiosaurus and its kin had flat, spatulate (leaf-shaped) teeth and possibly nostrils low on the head. *Mamenchisaurus* and other diplodocids had pencil- or peg-shaped teeth and nostrils high on the head. This may be related to how the dinosaurs fed – on soft, low-level plants, or on tough leaves from trees.

▼ This model of *Mamenchisaurus* displays the incredible neck. The middle part of the neck was probably not very flexible. Most of the bending took place just behind the head and near the shoulders.

Mamenchisaurus

Say it: Mam-en-key-sore-us
Dinosaur group: Diplodocid (Sauropoda, Saurischia)
When it lived: 150–140 mya, in the late Jurassic
Where it lived: Sichuan in China, and possibly Mongolia, Eastern Asia
Approx. size: Length 22 metres, height 8–9 metres, weight 7–10 tonnes
Special features: The longest neck of any dinosaur (in fact of any animal ever)

Mamenchisaurus and other diplodocids had peg-shaped teeth and nostrils set high on their heads.

Brachiosaurus and the other brachiosaurs had leaf-shaped teeth, and nostrils low on their heads.

▲ *Shunosaurus* had a bony lump at the end of its tail, armed with spines. This was probably swung, like a hammer or club, at enemies.

◀ The total length of *Mamenchisaurus* was about 22 metres. Almost half of this was the super-long neck. *Mamenchisaurus* could reach over 10 metres high, to feed on the leaves and shoots of conifer trees.

Armour and weapons

Saltasaurus was a medium-sized sauropod, about 12 metres long. Its remains were found in the Salta province of Argentina, South America, in 1980. They show two interesting things. One is that this sauropod lived right at the end of the Age of Dinosaurs, much later than most of its relatives, which lived in the Jurassic period. The other feature is that *Saltasaurus* may have had round, bony plates, about 10 centimetres across, in the skin of its back and sides. If so, this makes it the first armoured sauropod to be discovered.

The remains of another medium-sized sauropod, *Shunosaurus*, were found in Dashanpu Quarry, near Zigong in Sichuan province, China. At least ten of these 10-metre-long creatures were preserved in a mass grave, along with about 100 other dinosaurs. These included *Gasosaurus* (see page 29), some flying pterosaur reptiles and some fish. *Shunosaurus* was one of the few sauropods to have a defensive weapon – a tail-club to swing at attackers.

PLANT-EATERS

The rest of the dinosaurs in this book belong to the second great group of dinosaurs, the ornithischians, also called bird-hipped dinosaurs. Nearly all of these were plant-eaters. Some were small, light and swift. Others were huge and well-defended with spikes, horns and bony armour-plating on their body.

The ornithopods

The first main group of bird-hipped dinosaurs is the ornithopods, or 'bird-feet'. They include the hypsilophodonts, the iguanodontids like *Iguanodon*, and the hadrosaurs or 'duck-billed' dinosaurs. These dinosaurs all stood on their back legs and were herbivores. The name ornithopod is rather misleading, since the feet of these dinosaurs were not very similar to the feet of birds.

The hypsilophodonts were small to medium-sized ornithopods which first appeared in the late Jurassic period,

about 150 million years ago. More types evolved during the middle Cretaceous period, 120–110 million years ago.

The group is named after *Hypsilophodon*, whose remains include several well-preserved skeletons from the Isle of Wight, Great Britain.

▶ *Hypsilophodon* races away from a predator. At one time it was thought it lived in trees (see page 15).

◀ About twenty-three fossil skeletons of *Hypsilophodon* were found on the Isle of Wight. Some are almost complete, and preserved in great detail. They have the slim, long, light bones typical of a fast runner.

Cut-and-chew teeth

▼ *Tenontosaurus* was a large member of the hypsilophodont group, about 6 metres long and weighing up to 1 tonne (see also page 48).

The name *Hypsilophodon* means 'high-ridged tooth'. Its teeth were tall, sharp-ridged and close together, forming a long, saw-like edge that was ideal for cutting off and chewing leaves and other plant food. This dinosaur was only 2 metres long and very slim. It would have stood only waist-high to an adult human. Its main way of coping with predators was probably to dart away at speed into the undergrowth.

▲ *Dryosaurus* was a hypsilophodont about 4 metres long, that lived in North America and Africa about 140 million years ago. Like many ornithopods, it had no teeth at the front of its mouth. Instead, the predentary bone (see page 56) formed a 'beak' for nipping and clipping plant material.

Attacked by a pack

At one quarry site in western North America, fossils of a large hypsilophodont, *Tenontosaurus,* were found together with the remains of several of the 'terrible claw' theropods, *Deinonychus* (see pages 30–31). It is possible that the *Deinonychus* were hunting the *Tenontosaurus* in a group, like a pack of wolves. They would have leapt at *Tenontosaurus* and tried to slash open deep wounds with their foot-claws. They would have bitten their victim and torn it with their large-clawed hands. *Tenontosaurus* was probably big and heavy enough to fight off one *Deinonychus*, but not a pack of three or four which could have attacked from many directions at once.

Whatever happened, all the animals in this site perished in some natural disaster, perhaps a flood. Their bones could have been washed together by chance. They ended up in the same place and were slowly turned to stone, to be dug up 100 million years later.

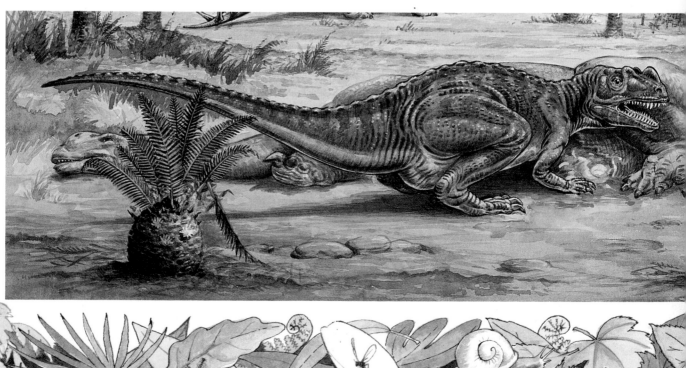

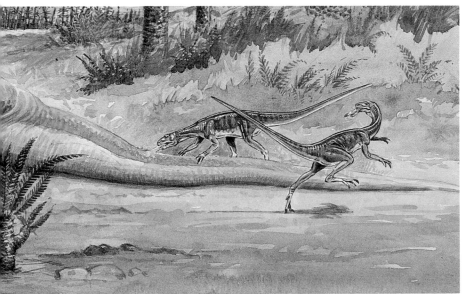

▲ A pack of *Deinonychus* ambush a *Tenontosaurus* in a ravine. The victim's main weapon is its powerful tail, which it is trying to swing at the attackers, and knock them off their feet.

◄ The carnosaur theropod *Ceratosaurus* (see page 22) feeds on the carcass of a sauropod, *Apatosaurus* (see page 42). Two coelurosaurs (see page 24), *Coelurus,* are also there, joining in the feast.

The finds on 'Egg Mountain'

Since 1978, fossil-hunters have been digging into the rocks near Bynum, Montana, USA. They have uncovered hundreds of dinosaur eggs and nests at a site now called Egg Mountain. Some of these belong to the hadrosaur *Maiasaura* (see page 58).

Others are from the 2-metre-long hypsilophodont *Orodromeus*. The nests of *Orodromeus* were spaced about 2 metres apart. Each consisted of a flat patch of ground where some fifteen to twenty eggs had been laid. Experts looked into the fossil eggs using machines usually used in medicine for scanning the inside of a human body. Inside the eggs they found baby dinosaurs which had not developed fully before being turned to stone.

Other eggs had clearly hatched and the babies gone. The shells lay broken and scattered around the nest site.

▶ A mother *Maiasaura* accompanies her youngsters away from the nest site. The first days and weeks after hatching would have been the most dangerous for the young – as it still is today.

◀ A model of the nest, eggs and newly-hatched babies of *Orodromeus*, which lived during late Cretaceous times. There is little sign of parental care. The babies would fend for themselves immediately.

Orodromeus

Say it: Orrow-droe-may-us (orrow like arrow)

Dinosaur group: Hypsilophodont (Ornithopod, Ornithischia)

When it lived: 80–70 mya, in the late Cretaceous

Where it lived: Montana, North America

Approx. size: Length 2–2.5 metres

Special features: Its fossil eggs in nests give information of dinosaur breeding behaviour; scans of eggs show developing embryos

The story of *Iguanodon*

The next main group of ornithopod dinosaurs includes *Iguanodon* and its relatives, such as *Ouranosaurus* and *Muttaburrasaurus*. They are known as the iguanodontids. *Iguanodon* itself holds a special place in the study of dinosaurs, partly because it was one of the first dinosaurs to be described, along with *Megalosaurus* (see page 28).

The first parts of *Iguanodon* to be discovered were some teeth. They were found near Lewes, Sussex, England, by Mary Mantell. She was the wife of Gideon Mantell, a doctor who studied fossils in his spare time. He recognized the teeth as unusual and showed them to experts of the time, such as William Buckland in Oxford (see page 28) and the great

▲ Fossilized footprints of an *Iguanodon* from 135 million years ago. They were found in Dorset, England.

French scientist Georges Cuvier. They thought that the teeth were probably those of a huge fish, or a mammal such as a rhinoceros.

Mantell was convinced that the teeth were very ancient, and that they were from a reptile. He noticed that they were similar in shape to the teeth of a living lizard, the iguana, though much bigger. In 1825 he wrote a scientific article saying that the teeth came from a huge, plant-eating, prehistoric lizard, 12 metres long. He called it *Iguanodon* or 'iguana tooth'. Soon the fossil remains of more of these 'giant lizards' were found. In 1842 the fossil expert Richard Owen suggested that they were not lizards, but a different kind of reptile. He proposed a new name for them – *Dinosauria* or the 'terrible reptiles'. And so began the study of dinosaurs.

▲ Mary Mantell, first finder of *Iguanodon* teeth. She is said to have picked up the teeth from a heap of road-mending gravel.

Plenty of fossils

Iguanodon is a much-studied dinosaur because hundreds of its fossil skeletons have been discovered across Europe and Asia. It was about 10 metres long and stood on its strong back legs. The large head and neck balanced the thick, powerful tail.

Iguanodon had a hard, horn-covered 'beak' at the front of its mouth for gripping and snipping off plant food. The lower part of the beak was made from a bone called the predentary bone, which is only found in ornithischian dinosaurs (see pages 47 and 56). At the back of the mouth were rows of wide teeth for chewing and grinding food into a pulp before it was swallowed.

◀ A meat-eating theropod dinosaur emerges from the trees and is spotted by the rearmost member of a small group of *Iguanodon*. Notice the similarity in body shape and posture between these different types of dinosaur.

Common herbivores

There is a gradual shift in the fossil record of plant-eating dinosaurs. From about the end of the Jurassic period, 140 million years ago, the huge, long-necked, four-legged sauropods (see page 38) seem to have been replaced by the two-legged dinosaurs like *Iguanodon* and its relatives. This happened particularly in Europe and Asia. Many hundreds of preserved iguanodontids from the middle of the Cretaceous period, 130–110 million years ago, have been unearthed. Such a large number of finds suggests that the *Iguanodon*-type dinosaurs were common creatures at the time. In their turn, they were replaced in some areas by another group of ornithopod dinosaurs, the hadrosaurs (see page 56).

Safety in numbers?

In 1878–81, deep in a coal mine near the village of Bernissart, Belgium, thirty-nine well-preserved *Iguanodon* skeletons were dug out. Collections of skeletons have been discovered at other places. There are also fossil footprints of several *Iguanodon*-type dinosaurs walking together, as there are for sauropods (see page 16). This evidence could mean that *Iguanodon* lived in groups or herds. These dinosaurs do not seem to have had any defensive armour or weapons, except for the spike-shaped claw on each thumb. Perhaps they relied on their fairly large size, and safety in numbers. The adults may have formed circles around the babies and youngsters, to protect them.

▼ *Ouranosaurus* had an extraordinary sail on its back. The sail could have absorbed the sun's heat quickly in the early morning. The dinosaur would therefore have been warmed up and active before its sail-less rivals and predators. So *Ouranosaurus* would have been first into action, giving it a head start in the struggle for survival.

▶ Instead of claws on its fingers and toes, *Iguanodon* had nail-like 'hooves'. The pointed 'hoof' on the thumb may have been a weapon used to stab enemies.

A spiny back

▼ *Muttaburrasaurus* roamed what is now Queensland, Australia, about 100 million years ago. Its fossilized remains were discovered in 1981. The bump on its nose is a puzzle. It does not seem to have had an obvious use. Perhaps it indicated the dinosaur's age and maturity to rivals and mates.

In 1966, the fossils of a strange iguanodontid came to light in Niger, north-west Africa. It took ten years to dig out the bones from the stones, clean them, and study and describe them in detail. (Ten years may seem a long time, but it is about average for large dinosaur remains.) This dinosaur was called *Ouranosaurus*, the 'brave reptile'. It was very similar to *Iguanodon*, although smaller, at 7 metres long. It had a curved 'sail' on its back which was held up by long thin strips of bone sticking up from the backbones. In life the sail was probably covered with skin. It may have worked as a heat-radiator, in the same way as the plates of another dinosaur, *Stegosaurus* (see page 80).

Dinosaurs down-under

For many years, dinosaur discoveries in Australia were few and far between. One of them was *Muttaburrasaurus*, which was named after the place of its discovery, Muttaburra in Queensland. It was a 7-metre-long iguanodontid and resembled *Iguanodon* in most details, except that it had a curious bony lump on the end of its nose.

In the late 1980s and early 1990s, amazing new finds were made at 'Dinosaur Cove' near Melbourne, in south-east Australia. These numerous fossils will provide exciting new information about dinosaurs, and they may change some of the ideas we now hold about the prehistoric world.

▶ *Camptosaurus* was one of the first and smallest iguanodontids. Its fossils come from several sites in North America and Europe.

The hadrosaurs

The last main group of ornithopod dinosaurs were the hadrosaurs, or 'duck-bills'. They are named from their beak-shaped mouth. This is formed by the front part of the jawbone, called the 'premaxilla', and the 'predentary bone', an extra bone at the front of the lower jaw (see also page 47 and page 53).

The predentary bone occurs only in ornithischian dinosaurs. In life, these bones were covered by hard horn, like a bird's beak. The horn grew all the time, so the 'beak' remained strong and sharp. A hadrosaur used it for pecking and nipping at plant food.

At the back of their mouth hadrosaurs had hundreds of diamond-shaped teeth arranged in rows. New teeth continued to replace old teeth all through the dinosaur's life. The sharp, sloping ridges of the teeth rubbed past each other to give a very powerful grinding action. Some hadrosaurs could munch the hard needle-leaves of conifer trees.

Edmontosaurus

Say it: Ed-mont-oh-sore-us
Dinosaur group: Hadrosaur (Ornithischia)
When it lived: 70–65 mya, in the late Cretaceous
Where it lived: Alberta (near Edmonton), Montana and Wyoming, North America
Approx. size: Length 12 metres, height 4–5 metres, weight 7–10 tonnes
Special features: Typical toothless beak at the front of the mouth; but up to 1,000 cheek teeth that were always being renewed, forming a powerful plant-grinding system

Skin and bone

Hadrosaurs lived towards the end of the Age of Dinosaurs, in the middle and late Cretaceous period. They were fairly large dinosaurs with powerful back legs. They stood on their back legs to eat plants.

Usually only the hard parts of living things form fossils. But sometimes soft parts such as skin and guts are preserved. Fossils of the hadrosaur *Edmontosaurus*, found in Wyoming, USA, include skin. The skin is still folded and wrinkled around the joints, just as it was in life.

◄ A herd of plant-eating hadrosaurs including 2 parasaurolophus (left), 2 lambeosaurs (in pool, right) and 4 corythosaurs (centre, front).

▲ This fossilized skin and bone is part of the chest and right arm of *Edmontosaurus*, and is some 67 million years old, about 2–3 million years before all dinosaurs died out.

▼ A fine fossilized skeleton of *Edmontosaurus*, part-buried in sandstone rock. It is about 70 million years old from Edmonton in Canada.

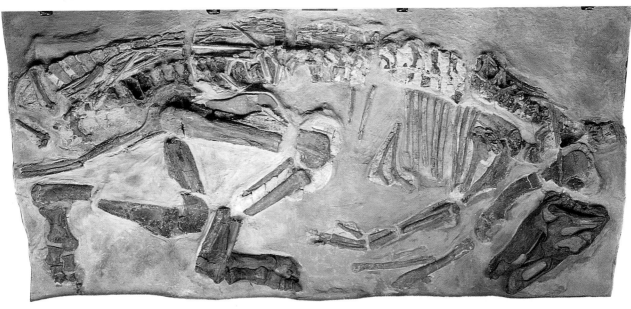

A 'good mother'

The series of discoveries in Montana, USA (see page 50) has changed people's ideas about dinosaurs. These finds challenged the view that mother dinosaurs simply laid their eggs and forgot about them. Dinosaur nests, containing hundreds of eggs and babies, were found in a place that became known as 'Egg Mountain'. Some nests belonged to *Orodromeus* (see page 50). Many nests belonged to the hadrosaur *Maiasaura*, the 'good mother reptile' (see also page 17).

The nests were about 7 metres apart – the same as the length of an adult *Maiasaura*. Each was a circular

mound of earth about 3 metres across and 1.5 metres high, with a hollowed-out bowl in the middle. In the bowl, the *Maiasaura* female laid eggs in circles, one layer on another. In some nests there were unhatched eggs. In other nests there were newly-hatched baby *Maiasaura*, only 50 centimetres long.
There were also fossils of larger youngsters, about 1 metre long, and some adults. From the structure of the nests, it seems that the dinosaurs came back to the same place to breed, year after year. The whole site is a dinosaur nursery frozen in time, and shows that some dinosaurs waited for their eggs to hatch and then looked after their babies.

Maiasaura

Say it: My-ah-sore-ah
Dinosaur group:
    Hadrosaur (Ornithischia)
When it lived: 75–65
    million years ago, in the
    late Cretaceous period
Where it lived: Montana,
    North America
Approx. size: Length 8–9
    metres, height 3 metres,
    weight 3–5 tonnes
Special features: The
    amazing numbers of
    fossils found suggest
    that there were vast
    herds of *Maiasura*;
    The nests, eggs and
    babies, preserved as
    fossils, teach us about
    their breeding
    behaviour

◀ About 75 million years ago, *Maiasaura* duck-billed dinosaurs return to their traditional nesting site. The old nests look like low volcanoes. Female *Maiasauras* probably rebuilt the nests, laid their eggs inside, and then perhaps covered the eggs with earth or vegetation, for warmth and protection.

Hadrosaurs with solid heads

There seems to have been two main types of hadrosaur. One contained the true hadrosaurs, or hadrosaurines. These had a flat head, or a strange-shaped crest of solid bone on top of the head. They included *Hadrosaurus* itself, *Anatosaurus*, *Edmontosaurus*, *Kritosaurus*, *Saurolophus* and *Maiasaura*. These hadrosaurines may have evolved from a dinosaur resembling *Iguanodon*.

The second group of hadrosaurs are the lambeosaurines (see page 62). These may have evolved from a dinosaur which resembled *Ouranosaurus* (see page 55). They also had extraordinary crests on their heads, but these were made of hollow bone.

The hadrosaurs evolved their amazing array of head-crests in a relatively short time. They also became common very quickly. One 'bone bed' in Montana, USA, contains the fossil remains of perhaps 10,000 *Maiasaura*. This may have been a vast, migrating herd, which was killed by poisonous gases and hot ashes from a nearby volcanic eruption.

Parasaurolophus

Say it: Para-sore-oh-loff–us
Dinosaur group: Lambeosaurine (Hadrosauridae, Ornithischia)
When it lived: 80–65 mya, in the late Cretaceous
Where it lived: Alberta, Utah and New Mexico in North America
Approx. size: Length 10 metres, height 3–4 metres, weight 5–8 tonnes
Special features: Hollow crest on top of up to 2 metres long, maybe used for a trumpeting call

▼ *Parasaurolophus* had the longest headgear of any hadrosaur. It is shown in more detail on page 62.

▼ *Tsinataosaurus* from China had a hollow tube that stood up between its eyes, and possibly pointed forwards.

▼ *Corythosaurus* wore a rounded head crest, like part of a large dinner plate.

▲ *Saurolophus* splashes in a pool. Fossils of this hadrosaur have been found in North America and Asia. The Asian versions are slightly larger with bigger crests.

Could the duck-bills swim?

One of the earliest hadrosaurs was *Bactrosaurus* from China and Mongolia. It lived 100–90 million years ago. It was one of the smallest hadrosaurs, at 4 metres long. The majority of hadrosaurs were 9–10 metres long. The largest were probably *Shantungosaurus* from China, at almost 15 metres, and *Lambeosaurus* from California, at up to 16 metres long.

   There is some evidence that the duck-billed dinosaurs could swim, or at least wade in deep water. The tails of several kinds, especially *Edmontosaurus*, *Shantungosaurus*, *Parasaurolophus* and *Lambeosaurus*, were tall and flat sided. The dinosaurs may have used their tail like a fish's tail – swishing it from side to side to push themselves through the water. They may also have used their paddle-shaped hands. We can imagine hadrosaurs swimming into deep water to escape predators. Only a few predators would have been big enough to tackle it, for example *Tyrannosaurus* and *Tarbosaurus*.

▲ *Saurolophus* hadrosaurs are chased into water by the carnosaur *Tarbosaurus*, an Asian version of *Tyrannosaurus* (see page 34).

Saurolophus

Say it: Sore-oh-loff-us
Dinosaur group: Hadrosaurine (Hadrosauridae, Ornithischia)
When it lived: 75–65 mya, in the late Cretaceous
Where it lived: Alberta and California in North America, Mongolia in Asia
Approx. size: Length 9–12 metres, height 2–4 metres, weight 4–8 tonnes
Special features: Asian beasts were much larger; possibly had a skin balloon on the nose

Were hadrosaurs noisy?

The head-crests of the hadrosaurs present a puzzle. The solid ridge along the snout of *Saurolophus* (see page 60) could have supported a loose patch of skin. The dinosaur could have blown this up like a balloon, making a honking or trumpeting sound. If the skin was brightly coloured, it would have flashed a visual signal, too. Many animals today use inflatable pouches to signal with sound and/or sight, such as some seabirds, seals and monkeys.

The lambeosaurine hadrosaurs included *Lambeosaurus*, *Corythosaurus* and *Parasaurolophus*. They had large, hollow crests which contained air tubes connected to the nose. By blowing or sucking through the tubes, these dinosaurs may also have been able to produce very loud bellows, trumpetings and other noises.

It is suggested that *Corythosaurus* could have sounded like a tuba or French horn, while the long crest of *Parasaurolophus* might have produced a noise like a noisy trombone!

▼ A lone *Parasaurolophus* walks near a marsh in North America, almost 70 million years ago. In this reconstruction, the long tube-shaped crest has a flap of skin like a 'flag'. This connects the crest to the neck and could have been a sight signal to others in the group.

► These *Corythosaurus* have been given bright-coloured skin by the artist. The skin on their head-plates shows up in the gloom, and helps the dinosaurs to see each other. Compare this reconstruction with the one on page 60, where the skin on the crest is brown. Even when skin has fossilized, its colour has never been preserved. So we can only guess the colour of dinosaurs.

▼ *Lambeosaurus lambei* had a two-part headpiece. The front part was hollow, and the rear-pointing spike was solid. If the colours in this reconstruction are correct, the crest may have helped to identify this dinosaur to other members of its group, and perhaps to rival herds of *Lambeosaurus*.

DINOSAUR HEAD-BANGERS

The pachycephalosaurs were a fairly small, strange group of bird-hipped dinosaurs which lived towards the end of the Cretaceous period, 90–65 million years ago. Their oddest feature was the enormously thick dome of bone on the top of their head, as though these dinosaurs were wearing bony crash-helmets!

The 'bone-domes'

The name pachycephalosaur means 'thick-headed reptile', and describes this group of dinosaurs perfectly. The skull bones on the top of their head, were amazingly thick and strong. In *Pachycephalosaurus*, the biggest of the group, the topmost curve of skull bone was over 30 centimetres thick. This has led to various nicknames for the pachycephalosaur group, such as the 'thick-heads', 'bone-heads' and 'bone-domes'.

▼ The skull of *Homalocephale* did not have a large dome of bone, but it did have a thickened roof of bone.

A lack of bodies

These domed skulls are the main fossils from the group, so far discovered. The hard, thick bone fossilized well. Only a few remains of other parts of skeletons have been found. So reconstructing a whole pachycephalosaur involves comparing the bone fragments with the remains of closely related dinosaurs, plus plenty of guesswork.

It seems that the pachycephalosaurs were sturdy plant-eaters which stood up and walked on their two strong back legs, in the same way as *Iguanodon* (see page 52). They varied in length from about 2 metres up to perhaps 10 metres.

Why so thick?

▼ *Pachycephalosaurus* was the largest of its group, at 8 metres long. *Homalocephale* (below left) was about 3 metres long, and *Stegoceras* (below right) only 2 metres long.

Why did the pachycephalosaurs have such tremendously thick top-knots? The main suggestion is that these dinosaurs used their head as a battering ram. A pachycephalosaur such as *Stegoceras*, the 'horny roof', would bend forwards so that its body was horizontal. Then it would run and charge head-first at something. The very deep, strong bone would not crack if it hit an object. The bone-dome would also protect the brain inside the skull from damage. In support of this view, the bones and joints in the neck and back seem to have been specialized for absorbing shocks and impacts.

◀ The skull of *Pachycephalosaurus* had a high lump of bone on top, and also smaller lumps and knobs around the sides. These may have been decoration with which to impress rivals and mates. The skull of *Stegoceras* is shown below.

◀ *Stegoceras* charges forwards in a head-butting pose. The thickened crown on its skull can be seen. Fossils of pachycephalosaurs such as *Stegoceras* come mainly from western North America and eastern Asia, with a few from England and Madagascar.

Using their heads

So what would a pachycephalosaur charge and head-butt? We can get clues from present-day animals. Some sheep and goats head-butt each other and they have thick skulls and also horns. It is mainly the males that do this, at breeding time. The pushing and butting is a trial of strength and stamina, to show their health and fitness. The winner takes charge of the group, and get to mate with the females.

It is quite possible that pachycephalosaurs lived in groups, in the same way as sheep and goats. Males may have had shoving and head-butting competitions with rivals. The victors would have mated with the females.

Males from neighbouring groups might have battled for females or perhaps for territory, in the same way. In addition, these dinosaurs could have used a battering-ram method to charge at enemies and predators, defending themselves and the group.

▲ *Pachycephalosaurus* walks in the Alberta woods. This was the largest of the pachycephalosaurs, and also the last of the group.

Pachycephalosaurus

Say it: Pack-ee-sef-ah-low-sore-us
Dinosaur group: Pachycephalosaur (Ornithischia)
When it lived: 70–65 mya, in the late Cretaceous
Where it lived: Alberta, North America
Approx. size: Length 8 metres, height 4 metres, weight 8–10 tonnes
Special features: Very deep dome of skull on the head, 25 cm thick; by far the largest pachycephalosaur

A family discussion

Where do the pachycephalosaurs belong in the dinosaur 'family tree' of evolution. It is fairly certain that they were ornithischians, or bird-hipped dinosaurs, because they had the predentary bone at the front of the lower jaw (see page 56). It is possible that they belong in the ornithopod group (see page 46), along with the hypsilophodonts (see page 46), iguanodontids (see page 52) and hadrosaurs (see page 56). They could also be put in the ankylosaur group of armoured dinosaurs (see page 76).

Or they could be put in as close relatives of the ceratopian group of horned and frilled dinosaurs (see pages 68–75). They then have the same importance as the other types – the ornithopods, ceratopians, ankylosaurs and stegosaurs. As with many other puzzles about dinosaurs, more fossil finds should help to decide the answer.

Stegoceras

Say it: Steg-oh-sair-ass
Dinosaur group: Pachycephalosaur (Ornithischia)
When it lived: 80–70 mya, in the late Cretaceous
Where it lived: Alberta, North America
Approx. size: Length 2 metres, height 1.5 metres, weight 60–70 kilograms
Special features: Thicker upper skull gave protection to the brain beneath; neck and spine also reinforced to take shocks of head–butting

▼ This skeleton of *Stegoceras* (see also page 65) displays its heavy skull and strong legs.

BEAKS, HORNS, SHIELDS AND FRILLS

The third main group of bird-hipped dinosaurs were the ceratopians, or 'horn-faces'. They had a brief but successful history towards the end of the Age of Dinosaurs. They were heavily built creatures that walked on all-fours. They had horns on their face, a parrot-beaked mouth, and large shields or frills of bone over their neck.

Fast-evolving variety

The ceratopians appeared about 90 million years ago. This was only 25 million years before the great extinction which ended the Cretaceous period, the Mesozoic era and the Age of Dinosaurs (see page 88). Yet during this relatively short period, many different kinds of ceratopians evolved. They had an extraordinary variety of face-horns and neck-shields or frills.

Large numbers of their fossil bones and skeletons have been discovered. One of the most famous of all dinosaurs, *Triceratops* (see page 74), was a ceratopian.

Most ceratopians lived in North America, but two of the earliest members of the group came from eastern Asia, chiefly Mongolia. These were *Protoceratops*, or 'first horn-face' and *Psittacosaurus*, or 'parrot reptile', (named after its beak-like mouth).

▲ A female *Protoceratops* kicks sand over the clutch of eggs she has just laid in her nest. This dinosaur had the ceratopian features of a parrot-beak mouth and large neck-shield, but it had no face-horns.

From small beginnings

Psittacosaurus dates from about 100–90 million years ago. It may represent an evolutionary link between the earlier ornithopod dinosaurs, such as *Hypsilophodon* (see page 47), and the main ceratopian dinosaurs. This is because *Psittacosaurus* had a combination of features from both groups. It was a fairly small dinosaur, only 2 metres long, and its general body shape and two-legged posture resembled the ornithopods. It did not have the face-horns and neck-frill of the later ceratopians, but it did have a ridge of bone along the back of the skull, and projecting bony parts in its cheeks. These could have been an early version of the face-horns and neck-frill.

◄ *Psittacosaurus* snips the leaves from a *gingko* (maidenhair) tree with its hard, beak-like mouth.

The fossils of *Protoceratops* are 80–70 million years old. This dinosaur had the heavy build and all-fours posture of the typical ceratopians. Like *Psittacosaurus*, it was quite small – 2 metres long and 180 kilograms in weight – about the same size as a large pig. *Protoceratops* became world-famous in the 1920s as the first dinosaur for which fossil eggs were found (see page 70).

▼ One type of *Protoceratops* skull had a light build, a small neck-shield and a smooth nose. The other was thicker and stronger, with a big neck-shield and a nose-bump. They may be female and male skulls.

▲ Rearing up on its back legs, *Psittacosaurus* would have been about as tall as an adult human. It may have used its long fingers for grasping and pulling plant food towards its mouth.

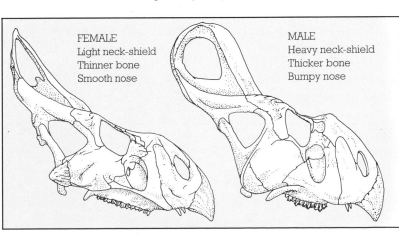

FEMALE
Light neck-shield
Thinner bone
Smooth nose

MALE
Heavy neck-shield
Thicker bone
Bumpy nose

▲ *Leptoceratops* was similar in size and general shape to *Protoceratops* (see page 68). But it lived in North America at a later time, 70 million years ago.

▶ The skull of *Leptoceratops* has no nose-bumps and only a small neck-shield. This ceratopian had a total length of about 2 metres.

▼ This reconstruction of *Centrosaurus* gives it a large, brightly coloured frill.

Eggs at last

For many years it was assumed that dinosaurs laid eggs like other reptiles. But there was no proof until the 1920s, when fossil-hunters in Mongolia discovered fossilized eggs laid by *Protoceratops.* Many eggs and nests were uncovered, as well as the fossilized remains of tiny babies inside the eggs. Each egg was about 20 centimetres long, shaped like a sausage, with a very thin shell.

Snip and cut

The upper, hooked part of the ceratopians' beak was made from a bone called the rostral bone, which only ceratopians had. The lower part was formed from the predentary bone (see page 56).

Ceratopian dinosaurs probably used their beak-mouths to snip off pieces of tough vegetation. They would have cut and chewed the pieces with their strong back teeth. This effective way of feeding may be one reason why the ceratopians were such successful dinosaurs.

▶ *Styracosaurus*, 'spiked reptile', was a short-frilled ceratopian (see page 72). The long spines on the frill must have looked very worrying to rivals and enemies. Complete skull and skeleton fossils of this dinosaur have been found in Alberta, Canada, and are dated at about 80 million years old. It was about 6 metres long.

Taking advantage

The ceratopian dinosaurs flourished after a new group of plants, the flowering plants, appeared about 120–100 million years ago. Before this time, the main plants were mosses, ferns, horsetails, conifer trees and cycads, which looked like dumpy palm-trees. The flowering plants may have resembled magnolia trees or water-lilies. They provided a new source of food, and the ceratopians, along with insects, may have been the first animals to take advantage.

The first large ceratopian to be discovered was *Monoclonius*, the 'single horn'. Its teeth were found in 1855 in Montana, USA. Better-preserved remains of a very similar dinosaur are called *Centrosaurus*, the 'sharp-point reptile'. It had a single horn sticking up from its nose, like that of today's rhinoceros, and perhaps two smaller horns pointing down from the top of the neck-frill. A marvellous selection of *Centrosaurus* fossils have been found in Alberta, Canada.

▲ This well-preserved skull of *Centrosaurus* is from Alberta, Canada. It is over 1.25 metres long. The whole skeleton is shown below left.

◀ *Centrosaurus* had a medium-sized neck-frill, and a very long single nose-horn.

Short and long frills

As the ceratopians changed and evolved, their nose-horns and their neck-shields or frills became larger and more elaborate. It is thought that the neck-shield may have started as a plate or collar of bone to anchor the very strong jaw-closing muscles

The later ceratopians can be divided into two groups, depending on the size and type of neck-shield or frill, and the number and position of the face-horns. One group is called the short-frilled ceratopians. This includes *Protoceratops*, *Styracosaurus*, *Leptoceratops* and *Centrosaurus*.

The other group covers the long-frilled ceratopians, which are all from North America. This group includes *Chasmosaurus*, *Anchiceratops*, *Torosaurus* and *Pentaceratops*.

The same but different

The variety of ceratopian heads, frills and horns illustrates a common problem for fossil experts. For example, the size and proportions of these features vary in some specimens of *Triceratops*. They all belonged to creatures of the same genus, *Triceratops*, but were they all the same species? Some experts believe the variations represent different species, such as *Triceratops horridus* and *Triceratops alticornis*. Others say they are all the same species, and show natural variation, as in species of animal alive today.

In such cases, there are other possibilities, which can cause further confusion. One is that there are two groups, male and female – and each of these shows natural variation within itself. Or the different groups represent juveniles and full-grown adults.

▼ *Chasmosaurus* was about 5 metres long. Its wide neck-frill had bony points, or 'nodules', around the edge.

► The largest member of the long-frilled ceratopian group was *Torosaurus*, the 'bull reptile', named from the two long cow-like horns above its eyes. The whole animal was over 7 metres long and weighed 3-4 tonnes. Its skull, which includes the neck-frill, was nearly 3 metres long – the largest head of any land animal that ever lived.

Saving weight

The long-frilled dinosaurs were among the last of the ceratopians. The first to appear was *Chasmosaurus*, the 'ravine reptile', some 80 million years ago. The neck-shield covered not only the neck, but the shoulders and front part of the body as well. If it had been solid bone, it would have been so heavy that the dinosaur would have been unable to lift its head. It was made lighter by holes in the bone, which were filled by skin, muscle and other soft tissues.

◄ *Pentaceratops* was one of the medium-sized ceratopians, at about 6–7 metres long, and with a weight of more than 5 tonnes. Here it snips and cuts leaves with its sharp, hooked, beak-like mouth, typical of the ceratopian dinosaurs.

◄ *Anchiceratops*, the 'close-horn face', sniffs the air for food and approaching danger. This long-frilled ceratopian was similar in size and build to *Chasmosaurus*. It had six spiky bones along the top edge of its frill, and also two bony lumps just below these, that pointed forwards.

Four-footed lumberers

The vertebral bones of the ceratopians were large and strong, as shown in the skeleton of *Centrosaurus* (see page 71). These were necessary to hold the weight of the huge skull and body.

Why did these dinosaurs have such extraordinary horns and frills? As mentioned earlier, a neck-plate or shield could provide a large surface for anchoring the powerful jaw-moving muscles. But there were probably other reasons, too. These are discussed along with the most famous ceratopian, *Triceratops*, on the next page.

Solid bone

Triceratops, the 'three-horn face', was the largest ceratopian dinosaur. It is also one of the most-studied. A tremendous find of about thirty *Triceratops* skulls was made in Wyoming, USA, allowing experts to study the variations in the size of the horns and neck-frills.

Scientists are still unsure as to whether *Triceratops* should be included in the long or the short-frilled group of ceratopians. The short-frilled types usually had a single nose-horn. The long-frilled types had three horns – one on the nose and two over the eyebrows. *Triceratops* had a combination of these features. It had a fairly small neck-frill and three face-horns. The neck-frill of *Triceratops* was solid bone, without the holes or 'windows' seen in the neck-frills of most other ceratopians.

Why grow horns and frills?

The neck-frill may have evolved originally to anchor jaw muscles (see page 72). But the astonishing variety and size of ceratopian frills and horns suggest that there were other reasons for having them.

One possibility is that they were used in self-defence. The neck-shield could have protected the dinosaur from the teeth and claws of predators. This seems likely in a dinosaur with a solid frill, such as *Triceratops*. But the large holes in the frills of other ceratopians would have made them much less protective.

Another possibility is that the ceratopian dinosaurs charged at predators and gouged them with their horns, in the same way that today's rhinoceroses charge enemies.

A third suggestion is that the elaborate horns and frill edges were a

sign of size, strength and maturity. This would have been especially important if the dinosaurs lived in social herds or groups. The ceratopians could have locked horns and had battles of power and stamina, to decide who was boss of the herd, and who would get to mate and produce offspring. If the frills and horns were covered with bright skin, they could also have acted as sight signals (see page 62).

Triceratops

Say it: Try-serra-tops
Dinosaur group: Ceratopian (Ornithischia)
When it lived: 70–65 million years ago, during the late Cretaceous period
Where it lived: Alberta, Saskatchewan, Montana, Colorado, South Dakota, Wyoming and other sites in North America
Approx. size: Length 8–9 metres, height 3 metres, weight 6–9 tonnes
Special features: Largest, heaviest, most common and most widespread of the horned dinosaurs; its neck frill was solid bone, unlike its frilled relatives

▲ The massive 2-metre skull of *Triceratops*.

▼ A mother *Triceratops* stands at bay, protecting her baby, with the rest of the herd in the background. Groups of fossils indicate that *Triceratops* lived in herds.

DINOSAURS IN SUITS OF ARMOUR

Another fascinating group of ornithischian dinosaurs were the
armoured ankylosaurs. Like the turtles and tortoises of today,
they were not fast or agile. They had bony plates, lumps, spikes
and spines over their bodies. These made them heavy and stiff,
but well-protected for life in the slow lane.

Plates and shields

▲ An early attempt at rebuilding *Polacanthus* put
the large spikes on the back facing upwards,
rather than sticking out from the sides.

The name ankylosaur means 'joined' or
'fused reptile'. It refers to the bony
plates, lumps, spines and nodules that
grew in the skin of these dinosaurs.
These bony parts were additional to
the usual bones of the skeleton inside
a dinosaur, and grew within the
thickness of the skin. They fused, or
joined together, to make large sheets,
casing and shields of bone. These
encased the dinosaurs in suits of
protective bony armour. The armour
was not as complete as that of their
reptilian relatives of today, the
tortoises, but was more like that of
the modern mammals, armadillos.

Heavy four-footers

The ankylosaurs were medium-sized dinosaurs that ate plants, like all of their ornithischian relatives. Because of the weight of their armour-plating, they walked on all-fours and they were probably slow and heavy-footed.

There were two main groups of ankylosaurs – the nodosaurids and the ankylosaurids (see page 78).

Nodosaurids

The nodosaurids lived about 130–90 million years ago. Their fossils have been unearthed in Europe and mid-western USA. One of the first dinosaurs to be discovered, *Hylaeosaurus*, was a nodosaurid. Its fossils came from Sussex, England, and were studied by Gideon Mantell (see page 52) in the 1830s.

Missing heads

The nodosaurids are named after *Nodosaurus*, the 'nodular (lumpy) reptile'. Its fossils were dug up in Wyoming and Kansas, USA, and date from around 100–90 million years ago. Another nodosaurid was *Polacanthus*, or 'many spikes', which was some 4.5 metres long. It lived 20 million years before *Nodosaurus*, on what is now the Isle of Wight, off the south coast of England.

Both of these creatures were well protected by plates and spikes of bone over their back and sides. But as neither set of fossils had a skull, they are usually reconstructed using the head of a similar nodosaurid from North America called *Panoplosaurus*.

▼ The skin of *Nodosaurus* contained rounded, bony lumps, arranged in bands. The whole creature was about 6 metres long.

▼ *Hylaeosaurus* was named 'woodland reptile' because its fossils were found in a forest. It was about 4 metres long.

▶ *Polacanthus* is known only from the rear part of its skeleton, while *Hylaeosaurus* is known only from its front part. It is quite possible that they were the same dinosaur.

Plates and planks

The second group of ankylosaurs were the ankylosaurids. Most of them lived during the middle or end of the Cretaceous period, 100–65 million years ago. They seem to have taken over from the nodosaurids in western North America and eastern Asia.

Two of the best-known ankylosaurids were *Euoplocephalus* the 'true plated head', and *Pinacosaurus* the 'plank reptile'. These names describe the arrangement of the armour of these dinosaurs. Ankylosaurids had fewer tall spines than their nodosaurid cousins, but they were more heavily armoured. The wide head was encased in bony shield-plates. Curved bands and strips of bone, bearing lumps and spikes, lay over the neck, back and sides. Some types even developed hard, bony, protective eyelids.

The largest of the ankylosaurids was *Ankylosaurus* itself, at up to 10 metres long, and weighing perhaps 4 tonnes. Like many of its relations, its fossils were found in Alberta, Canada, and Montana, USA. It was one of the last of the group, surviving right to the end of the Age of Dinosaurs, about 65–64 million years ago.

Self-defence

When in danger, an ankylosaurid could bend its legs and squat down on the ground so that a predator could not get at its unprotected underside. Trying to turn over one of these dinosaurs would have been like trying to tip over a tank.

Ankylosaurids also had a tail that ended in a heavy, bony 'club', which was probably used as a weapon. The ankylosaurid could have swung this into an enemy's legs.

▼ This is a view of the back of *Euoplocephalus*. You can see the remains of armour-plated skin. The fossil lacks a skull.

Confusing mixture

▼ *Pinacosaurus* was about 5 metres long. It lived in Mongolia in Asia. It had a horn-covered, beak-shaped mouth and weak cheek teeth with which it chewed plants. It would have swung its clubbed tail at any attacker.

The first remains of ankylosaurids were identified in 1902 in Alberta, Canada. They were found at sites along the Red Deer River. These sites have produced many fossils of numerous different dinosaurs, especially armoured ankylosaurs and horned ceratopians such as *Chasmosaurus* (see page 72). There was a confusing start to their study, with many names being given to different bits of fossils. Then fossil expert Lawrence Lambe realized that some of the remains, previously thought to come from different animals, were really from the same one, which he named *Euoplocephalus*.

◄ This reconstruction of *Euoplocephalus* shows the bony bands and studs of armour over its head, back and sides. The only unprotected part of this dinosaur was the underside.

SMALL BRAINS AND BIG PLATES

The final main group of ornithischian dinosaurs are the stegosaurs.
They had a tiny head, tiny teeth and a tiny brain. But they had
a huge body with huge plates of bone sticking up on the back.
They may seem unlikely creatures, yet their kind survived
for tens of millions of years.

A wide range

Stegosaurs walked on all-fours. They were heavily
built, plant-eating dinosaurs that lived mainly towards
the end of the Jurassic period, about 170–140
million years ago. The first fossils were discovered in
the 1870s in Oxfordshire, England, and were studied
by Richard Owen (see page 53). The most numerous
and most complete stegosaur fossils, of
Stegosaurus itself, were found in Wyoming and
Colorado, USA, in the 1870s and 1880s. Remains of
other stegosaurs from various dates in the Jurassic
and Cretaceous periods have been discovered at
several sites in western North America, also in
Britain, Europe, Africa, India and eastern Asia.

▲ *Kentrosaurus aethiopicus*
is well-named as the 'prickly
reptile'. The pieces of bone
on its back were shaped
more like spines than flat
plates. This dinosaur roamed
what is now Tanzania, Africa,
about 140 million years ago.

▶ Another reconstruction
of *Kentrosaurus* among the
massive *araucaria* and
conifer trees of the Jurassic
period. It was one of the
smaller stegosaurs, only
2.5 metres long, and about
as tall as a large pig.

Weak in the head?

Compared to its body, the head and brain of a stegosaur were tiny. *Stegosaurus* was a large dinosaur, 7 metres long and approaching 2 tonnes in weight. Yet its brain was only the size of a walnut. Despite this apparent 'stupidity', *Stegosaurus* was a long-lasting and successful type of dinosaur.

At first, the stegosaurs were thought to be armoured dinosaurs because of the large plates of bone found among the fossils. The fossils of *Stegosaurus* were put back together with the large plates flat over its back, like tiles on a roof. *Stegosaurus* means 'roofed reptile'.

Over the years, there have been many other suggestions as to exactly where and how the large plates fitted on this dinosaur's body. The modern view is that the plates stood upright on their wide base, arranged in two rows along the dinosaur's neck, back and tail. The plates in each row were not next to each other, but were offset, or staggered, with one row slightly behind the other.

▲ *Stegosaurus stenops* had long, pillar-shaped back legs, which meant its body sloped down to the head and tail.

Stegosaurus

Say it: Steg-oh-sore-us
Dinosaur group: Stegosaur (Ornithischia)
When it lived: 150–140 mya, in the late Jurassic
Where it lived: Colorado, Oklahoma, Wyoming in North America
Approx. size: Length 6–7 metres, height 2.5 metres (including upright back plates), weight 1.5–2 tonnes
Special features: Largest stegosaur; but one of the smallest dinosaur brains (thumb-sized)

Why have back plates?

What were the back plates for? They may have been covered with bright skin, as sight signals to show the sex, age and maturity of the owner. Another possibility is that they were 'heat exchangers'. Small details on the plates suggest that they were covered by skin with a very rich blood supply. In the early morning, after the cool night, the stegosaur would stand out in the sun and absorb heat through the large surfaces of its plates. In this way, it warmed up and became active faster than a similar dinosaur without plates. It could therefore feed sooner and for longer. If the stegosaur became too hot, the plates could also give off body heat and cool it down.

◀ *Stegosaurus* might have stood like this to face an attacker. The plates would have protected its head and neck, as it swung its spine-covered tail at the enemy.

▼ Fossils of *Tuojiangosaurus* come from China and are about 150 million years old. This was a medium-sized stegosaur, 5–6 metres long.

▲ *Stegosaurus* is the largest of the known stegosaurs, reaching lengths of about 7 metres. It has only been found in North America so far.
◀ *Kentrosaurus,* about 2.5 metres long, lived in Africa (see also pages 80–81). Its fossils come from the same site, Tendaguru in Tanzania, as the huge sauropod *Brachiosaurus* (see page 40).

THE DINOSAURS' RELATIVES

In a great catastrophe, about 65 million years ago, all the dinosaurs
died out, along with many other living things (see page 88).
But the dinosaurs may have left some descendants.
A group of creatures that may have evolved from dinosaurs in the
Jurassic period are still flourishing today – the birds.

Mistaken identity

In 1951, a fossil skeleton from the Solnhofen area of Bavaria, Germany, was identified as the small theropod dinosaur *Compsognathus* (see page 25). They were then put into the collections of the Eichstätt Museum.

In 1973 the fossils were studied again. The experts realized that they were not from *Compsognathus*. They were not from a dinosaur – or even a reptile – but were, in fact, from a bird. So they were renamed *Archaeopteryx*, 'ancient wing'. *Archaeopteryx* was the first known bird. It lived in the middle of the Jurassic period, about 160–150 million years ago. So far, seven sets of fossils have been discovered, all from the same area of Germany. The first was a single feather, found in 1861.

This case of mistaken identity shows how similar the early birds were to the small theropod dinosaurs such as *Compsognathus*. It is possible that *Archaeopteryx* evolved from this type of dinosaur, and therefore represents a very early stage in bird evolution. But some people argue that it was a reptile, not a bird.

◄ *Hesperornis,* in the foreground, was a seabird from the late Cretaceous period. It resembled birds of today called divers. Flying past in the background are *Nyctosaurus* pterosaurs (winged reptiles).

Part reptile, part bird

Archaeopteryx was 50 centimetres long overall, with a body roughly the size of a modern crow. It was an amazing half-way animal – part reptile and part bird. Much of it was very similar to a small theropod dinosaur, and not similar to a bird. It had teeth; modern birds have no teeth. It had bones in its tail; modern birds have only feathers in their tail. It had three 'fingers' tipped with claws on its wings; modern birds do not.

But *Archaeopteryx* had bird features too. Its front legs were wings. It had a furcula, or wishbone, to strengthen its shoulders. This would have provided attachments for muscles used in flight. And it had feathers, the possession of which is the main feature of a bird. No other creature has feathers. The shapes and details of the feathers can be seen in some of the *Archaeopteryx* fossils.

▲ *Archaeopteryx* glides after an insect in a Jurassic woodland. It could probably flap its wings, but it was not a strong flier.

▼ One of the world's most valuable fossils – *Archaeopteryx* in marvellous detail. The wings and feathers fan out on the upper left and right. The legs are below, the tail on the lower left, and the skull faces to the left.

Taking to the air

There are two main ideas as to why birds took to the air. One is that they climbed into trees and then leaped and glided down to chase flying insects for food, or to escape from predators. The other is that they ran along the ground and jumped into the air, again to catch flying insects. Feathers may have evolved as a light, smooth wing surface to help the animal fly. Or they could have started as an insulating, heat-retaining 'blanket' for a warm-blooded animal, in the same way that mammals' fur developed.

Another suggestion is that feathers began as a lightweight 'net' on the creature's arms, which it swung out to catch small insects for food. In the case of the 'blanket' and 'net' ideas, the use of feathers in flying was only a secondary one.

▲ Two *Avimimus portentosus* battle over a lizard. *Avimimus* may have had feathers! Tiny bumps on its preserved arm bones could be attachment points for feathers.

Avimimus

Say it: Ave-ee-mim-us
Dinosaur group: A small theropod of uncertain relationships (Saurischia)
When it lived: 75–70 mya, in the late Cretaceous
Where it lived: Mongolia, Eastern Asia
Approx. size: Length 1.5 metres, height 80–100 centimetres, weight uncertain (a few kg?)
Special features: Some controversial studies suggest the arms and possibly other parts were feathered.

Bird evolution

There are few fossils of other birds from the Jurassic period. Bird bones are very thin and fragile, to save weight for better flying, and tend to get broken before they can be fossilized. However, there are remains of birds from the Cretaceous period.

After the death of the dinosaurs and other creatures, 65–64 million years ago, birds flourished. Some of them became enormous. About 50 million years ago, a huge bird called *Diatryma* stalked North America. It had tiny wings and could not fly. But it was more than 2 metres tall, with strong back legs for running, and a massive hooked beak for tearing up prey.

▼ This scene shows the types of animal alive during the late Cretaceous period, in what is now Montana, USA.

Deinosuchus, a huge crocodile 15 metres long, lurks in the swamp. Crocodiles began their history at about the same time as dinosaurs.

Several birds stand on the near shore, and one poses boldly on the crocodile's head. They are *Ichthyornis*, the 'fish bird', similar to the terns and gulls of today.

Archaeopteryx

Say it: Ark-ee-op-tur-icks
Bird group: Archaeornithes
When it lived: 150–130 million years ago, during the late Jurassic period
Where it lived: Southern Germany, Europe
Approx. size: Length 30–40 centimetres, wingspan 40–50 centimetres, weight 300–400 grams
Special features: The earliest known bird by many millions of years; shows a 'jigsaw' combination of reptile and bird features

Flying to the right are two pterosaurs (winged reptiles) which were cousins of the dinosaurs. They shared the air with the birds and insects.

On the far shore, a small herd of *Kritosaurus* hadrosaurs (see pages 56 and 60) hurry through the sunlit trees.

THE END OF AN ERA

About 65 million years ago, there was a world-wide disaster.
Many kinds of animal and plant became extinct.
That means they died out for ever. They included dinosaurs,
pterosaurs, many sea reptiles, curly-shelled ammonites, and
many small animals and plants in the plankton of the oceans.

The great extinctions of 65 million years ago happened very quickly in terms of Earth's whole history. They marked the end of the Cretaceous period and the Mesozoic era, or 'Middle Life' (see pages 10–11).

Many suggestions have been made to explain the mass extinctions. Perhaps a giant meteorite from space crashed into Earth and threw up a huge cloud of dust that blotted out the Sun for many years. In the gloom, plants would have withered and died, and animals would have run short of food.

Perhaps many volcanoes erupted at about the same time, pouring out poisonous fumes and clouds of ash which blocked the sunlight and smothered the land and sea.

Perhaps the climate changed rapidly, and some animals and plants could not evolve quickly enough to survive. But none of these theories explain why certain animals died out while others, such as the crocodiles, turtles, birds and mammals, survived.

Whatever the reason, the dinosaurs, rulers of the land for 140 million years, were gone. The Mesozoic era was followed by the Cenozoic era, or 'Recent Life'. This became the Age of Mammals and Birds, and still continues today.

▼ Mammals appeared at about the same time as dinosaurs. But throughout the reign of the dinosaurs, mammals were small and insignificant. This is a model of the 10-centimetre-long, shrew-like *Megazostrodon*. It was one of the first mammals, from about 200 million years ago.

▲ A pterosaur flaps across the evening sky as a meteorite smashes into Earth. The impact of a huge meteorite is one theory for the mass extinctions at the end of the Cretaceous period.

▼ A herd of *Maiasaura* try to run from a vast rolling cloud of ash, thrown into the air during massive volcanic eruptions. This is another possible explanation for the mass extinctions.

FIND OUT SOME MORE

USEFUL ORGANIZATIONS

One of the best ways to find out about dinosaurs and other prehistoric creatures is to go fossil-hunting. Find out about your local natural history society or geological society. They may organize fossil study days. Your local library will have a list of such societies. These organizations will also help you:

RockWATCH, The Green, Witham Park, Waterside South, Lincoln LN5 7JR. This recently-formed subsection of WATCH, which is the junior branch of The Wildlife Trusts (formerly the Royal Society for Nature Conservation), runs meetings all over the country.

The Geologists Association, Burlington House, Piccadilly, London W1V 0JU. They will be able to give you more information about local geological societies, and could suggest what to do and where to go.

The Dinosaur Society, 84 Moffat Road, Waban, Massachusetts 02168, USA. This society works to promote accurate scientific information about dinosaurs. They co-operate in the publication of Dino Times, a monthly newspaper for children.

INTERESTING BOOKS

If you want to read some more about dinosaurs and other prehistoric animals, you will find these books interesting:

Cambridge Field Guide to Prehistoric Life by David Lambert (Cambridge University Press, 1989)

Collins Guide to Dinosaurs by David Lambert (Collins, 1983)

Dinosaur (Dorling Kindersley, 1990)

Dinosaur! by Dr David Norman (Boxtree, 1991)

Dinosaurs, a global view by S. J. Czerkas & S. A. Czerkas (Dragon's World, 1990)

Fossils in Colour by J. F. Kirkaldy (Blandford Press, 1980)

The Macmillan Illustrated Encyclopedia of Dinosaurs and Prehistoric Animals by D. Dixon, B. Cox, R. Savage and B. Gardiner (Macmillan, 1988)

The Pocket Guide to Fossils by Chris Pellant (Dragon's World, 1992)

PLACES TO VISIT

Most large museums have displays of fossils, and many of them have dinosaur exhibitions. These are some of the best around the country:

Dorchester Dinosaur Museum, Icen Way, Dorchester, Dorset (this is the only museum in Britain devoted exclusively to dinosaurs, with lots of exhibits that you can actually touch)

Geology Museum, High Street, Sandown, Isle of Wight (features an exhibition of recently excavated dinosaurs)

Leicestershire Museum, New Walk, Leicester (includes a local dinosaur display)

National Museum of Wales, Cathays Park, Cardiff (includes a collection of Welsh fossils and dinosaur skeletons)

Natural History Museum, Cromwell Road, London SW7 (this museum has the most comprehensive dinosaur exhibition in Britain, and a huge collection of fossil plants and animals)

Oxford University Museum, Parks Road, Oxford (houses a good collection of fossil bones and a plaster cast of a dinosaur skeleton)

Royal Museum of Scotland, Chambers Street, Edinburgh (important collections of fossils and minerals)

Sedgwick Museum of Geology, Downing Street, Cambridge (this museum has fossil fragments of around a dozen dinosaurs, as well as plaster reconstructions of some dinosaurs)

INDEX